Paris–Roubaix:
The Inside Story

All the bumps of cycling's cobbled classic

Les Woodland

McGann Publishing
Cherokee Village, Arkansas

Photo credits: page 105 and back cover Les Woodland; page 136 Bill McGann; all other photos are from the collection of and copyright Fotoreporter Sirotti, and are reprinted with his permission.

Published by McGann Publishing
P.O. Box 576
Cherokee Village, AR 72525
USA
www.mcgannpublishing.com

McGann
Publishing

ISBN 978-0-9859636-1-3
Printed in the United States of America

Cover photo: riders in the 2007 Paris–Roubaix on the Moulin de Vertain cobble sector.

"Better to reign in hell than to serve in heaven."

Paradise Lost, John Milton (1608–1674)

Men transformed into dusty or mud-caked zombies locked in a battle for survival. Their machines, submitted to the traps of a demented road, fall prey to repeated technical incidents. The falls, individual or collective, open the pages of a perpetual tragedy.

—Vélo Magazine, 2004

Introduction

One of the world's least inviting bike rides follows the western European coast from the cold north towards the warmer south. Then, just as you hope the weather will improve, it crosses to England and goes north again. It's a chilly ride because it circuits the gray, gloomy North Sea. And the North Sea is never a place of parasols and hula girls.

It was out on the North Sea in the Seventies that a ship called the *Mi Amigo* housed an unlicensed pop radio station of the same name. It was run by a Belgian waffle entrepreneur. He never saw why everybody else thought that so funny. Radio Mi Amigo played commercials for anyone but especially it advertised Suzy waffles. Those who hadn't already giggled succumbed when they heard they were named after the waffle-maker's wife... from whom he shortly separated.

The station had enormous audiences in Holland and Belgium, where they heard the advertisements and which—being in Dutch—they understood. One of the ads included the excited voice of a Belgian sports commentator.

"Daar komt-ie, de sterkste, de winnaar—MARC DEMEYER WINT PARIJS–ROUBAIX!" he screamed. In the background the crowd went wild, for Roubaix is close to the Belgian border and Belgians climb into their red-numbered cars and drive over the border and feel close to home.

Demeyer won—if you believed the ads—by chewing Stimorol gum. But it didn't do him much good. He died shortly afterward of a heart attack as he sat doing a crossword puzzle in front of his television. He was 32. And Sylvain Tack—Mr Suzy Waffles—also came to an unhappy end. New laws put an end to his radio station and an encounter with customs officials in Paris put an end to his liberty—for smuggling three kilograms of cocaine. He died at home in Oudenberg in February 2006, a sad and broken recluse.

Belgians have long seen Paris–Roubaix as theirs. The greatest of them all was Roger De Vlaeminck, a gypsy-looking man who more drifted than bounced across the cobbles. Belgians like Paris–Roubaix because it matches their Tour of Flanders, the Ronde van Vlaanderen, which also has as many cobbles as the organizers can find. Spectators come into France and wait until Paris–Roubaix has passed and then prize up a cobblestone to take home. A group of enthusiasts called *Les Amis de Paris–Roubaix* does its best to replace them but there are always plenty enough missing cobbles to give the race a bike-breaking, back-breaking quality that excites some and scares many.

Two novice rookies were once listed to ride. They'd seen it on television and they'd heard of the broken bones. They'd seen the race riding slippery, mud-covered cobbles at speeds greater than they cared to imagine. They'd seen riders and bikes snapping in watery holes. They spent a sleepless night in their hotel. And next morning they went back home.

Anybody could see why. Who would face six or seven hours of purgatory and the serious risk of a broken leg—for such things have happened—to be no better than an also-ran, an also-fallen? For the tailenders don't get even a ride round the track at the finish—because that's open only to the first arrivals.

Bernard Hinault dismissed Paris–Roubaix as *une cochonnerie de course*, which isn't easy to translate but is unflattering. Not that that stopped his winning in 1981. Jacques Anquetil, frustrated by a flat tire 13 kilometers from the end in 1958, called it "a dangerous lottery." Others, like De Vlaeminck, made a career of it. Some, said Stephen Roche, "would kill their own mother to get on the podium." It's what Jacques Goddet called "the last great madness of cycling." It should live, he said, for that reason alone.

They call Paris–Roubaix the "Hell of the North". The American writer James Startt tells of an American television crew reporting it for the first time.

"They were relieved to find a key figure in the race, Theo De Rooy, who could speak English," he wrote. "What made the race memorable was De Rooy's early break, a planned sacrifice that somehow put him in a position to win. But as he seized this chance of a lifetime, he flatted and crashed while in the lead, finishing a long way from first.

"No sooner was De Rooy off his bike than the CBS crew jumped on him. His haggard face was covered with mud and blood when they asked for his race impressions. He was so exhausted he could hardly speak, but he muttered something about how hard and heartbreaking Paris–Roubaix could be."

What he is actually said to have muttered demonstrates the command of English you'd expect of a former world university champion: "It's a bollocks this race! You're working like an animal, you don't have time to piss, you wet your pants. You're riding in mud like this, you're slipping, it's a piece of shit…"

He sounded so miserable and the CBS people were so new to the race that the reporter, John Tesh, asked if he would ever ride again.

De Rooy's face transformed. "Ride it again?" he asked. "Of course I will. This is the most beautiful race in the world."

Complete known results for every edition of Paris–Roubaix can be found on the publisher's website, www.BikeRaceInfo.com

Today we are visiting a world that would have been forgotten if one day a bike race hadn't had this crazy idea, once a year, of turning left on the way out from Troisvilles, leaving the civilization of the car to plunge into the meandering history of the Nord. The names are devilishly evocative: Inchy, Verchain–Maugré, Quérénaing. They are the first stations of the cross. You couldn't invent something like that.

—Philippe Bouvet, *L'Équipe*, 2006

1

To a Cyclist, It's Beautiful

You have a lot of trouble selling your wares if you make beer, cigarettes or running shoes. You're either not allowed to say what they do—"Drink our beer and it'll make you drunk"—or there's not enough space on the page to try. So it is with running shoes. A while back, one company tried a different approach. It heaped a dozen battered, stained and sweat-stained shoes and beneath them wrote: "To a runner, they're beautiful."

And so it goes for the town of Roubaix. For cyclists it is the end of the rainbow. For the rest of France, it is an embarrassment, a run-down place so close to Belgium that you wonder they don't push it across the border. If an enemy again invaded, nobody would defend Roubaix.

What's surprising is that somewhere that means so much to cyclists counts for so little in the country that made it famous. Because Roubaix now isn't so much a town in its own right, although that's its status, but a suburb of Lille. Things aren't always wonderful in Lille, either, but it has risen and it was 2004's European capital of culture. It has history—Charles de Gaulle was born there, for instance—and it has status. It is the number one town of the Nord region, a business center, a city of a quarter of a million. Its mayor, Martine Aubry, is of national status in French politics.

And then, tucked on its side, is Roubaix. You get there by bus or by train. The rail station is a charmless platform of faded paint and broken lamps. You sense the trains from there to neighboring Kortrijk—Courtrai to the French—are grateful to slip into Belgium.

Roubaix is a daughter of the industrial age. It had 8,090 residents in 1800. In 40 years they reached 24,800 and half a century later there were 115,000. Countryside still separated it from Lille to the southwest and from Belgium. But cows that grazed there were strangers to clean air. Roubaix was a textile town. The French had begun calling it the Manchester of France or *la ville aux mille cheminées*—the town of a thousand chimneys. The smoke blew out over the shabby homes of textile workers and on towards the cows.

Roubaix bristled with resentment. At school, children of seven drilled with fake arms to never again suffer the ignominy of German invasion. In 1870 the Germans had shelled Paris and laid siege for four months. Parisians had resorted to eating rats—and the two elephants in the zoo—before the city collapsed. France had lost Alsace-Lorraine. *Jamais encore ça*, the children chanted: we'll never suffer that again.

Their indignation followed that of their parents. This was the 19th century and French mill owners were like capitalist colleagues elsewhere. They lived in luxury with little concern for employees. Ten per cent of the population had ninety per cent of the money. Their workers toiled 10 hours a day for six days a week. They worked in deafening noise, breathing air poisoned by dyes and bleaches. Those injured as they worked were fired and sent away. Their usefulness was over.

Roubaix treated 5,000 tons of wool in 1881, soaring to 190,000 by 1908. The town needed all the workers it could get and people came from neighboring towns, from the farms and from Belgium. The law insisted children study until 13. In industrial Roubaix, the last thing families wanted was children at school. What was the point of an education when the only prospect was work in a factory? Families needed money and food, not learning. Children followed their fathers into the mill as soon as they were tall enough for bosses to turn a blind eye. And turn a blind eye, they did—it was cheaper to employ children than adults.

Their miseries were crystallized by the rue des Longues-Haies, a pretty name—the Road of Long Hedges—which added black humor to the conditions. Where the name came from, I have no idea. But the nearest to black hedges there in the 19th century were the long lines of continuous, smoke-darkened tenement houses that stood there. Still stand there.

You can still walk along what remains of the rue des Longues-Haies, for much of it has been demolished. It's the rue Édouard Anseele these days, named after a Belgian socialist, in the corner of the boulevard

Gambetta and the rue Pierre de Roubaix. A long brick wall runs on one side, giving an idea of factories that stood there. At number 28, for instance, Motte Porisse made wool for the Chat Botté company; further along at 38 was a factory making household fabrics; then came the Motte Bossut works and, further along, the Lemaire et Dillies concern that made bed covers. At the far end, in the part of the road that still stands, were several hat-makers.

The fronts of the houses have for the large part been renovated, clumsily modernized, but the brickwork of upper stories looks authentic. Brick picks it out as northern France: brick is rare in the rest of the country. The road, lined now with cars on one side, is just wide enough for 19th century motorized carts to pass. I call them that because "truck", the modern word, overstates the case.

The houses were built as an investment by smaller businessmen—shopkeepers, lesser manufacturers—and as inexpensively as possible. They had no indoor lavatory and no bath. Not until the summer of 1911 did the rue des Longues-Haies have a bathhouse, a large tiled room where the grimy sat on benches to wait their turn. The rules forbade customers to wash their clothes and sheets, but many did. The baths closed only on the last day of 1960.

The rue des Longues-Haies is written into French social history for the rat-like conditions of families who lived there, the men working in mills, the women sewing at home or working in the astonishing 2,400 bars of the neighboring streets. The families inherited nothing, possessed nothing and left nothing. They were owned, in practice if not fact, by the mill owners. Sirens summoned them to work and told them when to go home. Those who didn't work by day worked all night instead.

The mills have long since closed. You can still see them, though, cleaned up, sanitized and used as offices or shopping centers. Half close your eyes and you think you can picture how they must have looked then, but nothing brings back the stench, the noise, the poverty.

Such a background produced lively politics. Those who represented the élite rarely agreed with those elected by the humble. The humble succeeded in electing Henri Carette, the first *collectivist* mayor in France. These days we'd call him a communist, and communism remains a force in northern France.

Carette's views hardly accorded with those of Théo Vienne and Maurice Perez but all three did a lot for the workers of Roubaix. Vienne and Perez had a textile mill in the rue du Pays. From the old rue des Longues-Haies, you walk west to the rue Pierre de Roubaix, cross the large road junction at the next block and continue into what's now the avenue des Nations-Unies. Follow it as it bends left and then turn left into the sweetly- named avenue de la Fosse aux Chênes—avenue of the oak-lined ditch. Vienne and Perez had their mill in the first turning on the right, where the Red Cross stands now.

Vienne, the livelier of the two, was a gentle-faced man with a fashionable drooping mustache wider than his jaw and sharp, observant eyes. Roubaix was his home and where he'd been born, in 1864. He

Théo Vienne: "I have a dream…"

and Carette agreed that sport was good for the masses. Their reasons may have been different—Carette saw sport as social advancement and a way of keeping men from alcohol, while the mill owners considered it a way to keep employees strong and healthy and out of socialist and union meetings—but they did agree.

In other ways, they differed. Carette helped found the *Fédération Cyclopèdique du Nord* in 1890 as a contribution to society; Vienne promoted boxing, wrestling and bullfighting as a contribution to his wallet. The *New York Times* called him the leading fight promoter in France. On July 14 in 1899, France's national holiday, he packed his bullring by announcing a duel between a bull and a lion. In less kindly times, it was a sensation. *La Vie au Grand Air,* the news magazine of the day, spoke of 10,000 enthusiasts arriving by train. They went home disappointed. *Le Vélo,* which went beyond cycling, reported: "They wanted the horrible and they didn't get it." The animals simply ignored each other.

Vienne and Perez were cyclists, not uncommon in society at the time. Vienne was president of the *Sport Vélocipèdique Roubaisien* and Perez president of the *Cercle Vélocipèdique Roubaisien,* two of the town's four clubs. They had seen and some say they had organized races in the beautiful Parc Barbieux, a long strip of land radiating from the center of Roubaix and crossed by paths and water. The enthusiasm of cyclists on barely controllable machines was rarely to the liking of those walking there and taking the air.

The two mill owners saw the possibilities. Anybody could watch races in a park for nothing; put them in an arena and money could change hands. And so, in some measure for profit but also as a contribution to the city which had made them "fabulously rich", according to one account, they bought 46,000 square meters at the junction of the rue Verte and the route de Hempempont. There they would build a vélodrome. Its position beside the Parc Barbieux was fortunate but more deliberate was the closeness to the Mongy, the tramway that could bring in spectators from Lille. Those traveling from further could arrive by rail at nearby Croix-Wasquehal.

Vienne and Perez engaged a lawyer called Duchange and created the *Société Anonyme du Vélodrome de Roubaix.* They registered it in Croix, a suburb of Roubaix, with a capital of 160,000 francs. Through the company they sold shares in their venture to whoever would help raise the cost. Many went for five francs apiece.

Vienne and Perez knew every businessman and contractor in town and they chose a builder and an architect, Élie Derveaux, who promised to complete the job in two months. Work started at the beginning of April 1895 and around a hundred workmen had completed the job by the end of May. Roubaix had a vélodrome. It had taken 300,000 bricks and the shifting of 6,000 cubic meters of earth and the erection of a great number of flagpoles. It stood, a curve of brick with high domed windows on the outside, in a field of grass churned to mud by workmen and then by spectators. Dunlop, the tire company, bought advertising where it could. Pneumatic tires were still a novelty: the company had started only six years earlier.

The mill owners knew not only their workers, they knew their sport. *La Bicyclette* in May 1893 had said, admittedly not without bias, that: "Of all sports in our region of the Nord, the most popular by far today is cycling." The evidence, said the writer, was not only the cyclists he saw out "devouring kilometer after kilometer" on the road but the fact that neighbouring Lille was building a vélodrome next to its horse-racing circuit.

Roubaix's track—333.33 meters round and made with 140 tons of cement, with suspended bankings (an architectural first) that rose 37 centimeters each meter—opened on Sunday, June 9, 1895, a day of magnificent sunshine. Buses were laid on all afternoon from the town center. Close on 90 riders took part in the opening races, including a talented local star called Maurice Garin, still eight years from winning the first Tour de France.

The problem was that Roubaix was 280 kilometers from Paris. The capital was not simply France's administrative center but a whirlpool drawing in every bubble of talent and initiative. France was a centralized society and its hub was Paris. Roubaix, already in the shadow of Lille, was on the Belgian border. Geographically, politically and culturally, it couldn't be further away. Just how great that distance and ignorance was gave rise within two decades to the term "Hell of the North".

The idea of a race from Paris to Roubaix was novel because few knew Roubaix and still fewer cared and because every other race of importance went *to* Paris and not *from* it. The first road race, won by

James Moore, had gone from Paris to Rouen. But thereafter anything that mattered finished where everything mattered: in Paris. The longest of them, Bordeaux–Paris, was 560 kilometers. You couldn't ride it without a lot of preparation. And so in February 1896 Vienne and Perez wrote to Paul Rousseau, the imposing and mustachioed director of *Le Vélo*, which had taken over its organization.

"Dear Monsieur Rousseau,

"Bordeaux–Paris approaches: the great annual challenge founded by *Véloce-Sport* and entrusted for the past year to *Le Vélo*, has done so much to spread the word of cycling that an idea has come to us. What would you think of a training race three weeks before Bordeaux–Paris?

"Paris–Roubaix would entail a course of about 289 kilometers, which would be nothing for participants in Bordeaux–Paris. The finish could take place on the vélodrome Roubaisien with several laps of the track, as for the finish of Bordeaux–Paris at the Seine [track]. The crowd would welcome each rider enthusiastically, all the more so because the people of Roubaix have never seen the spectacle of a great road race. And we know enough track riders here to know that Roubaix would show true hospitality.

"As for prizes, we offer here and now a first prize of 1,000 francs in the name of the Vélodrome Roubaisien and we'll occupy ourselves by raising more prizes so that everyone will be satisfied.

"As for the date, we think May 3 would fit perfectly because the riders in Bordeaux–Paris will already be in good shape by then and they'll have three weeks to recover before the big race.

"And so, *cher Monsieur*, can we count on the support of *Le Vélo*, on your expertise for the organization, the start, etc? If so, announce the *great event* [in English in the letter] straight away and open your columns to entries.

With our friendly greetings…

Théo Vienne and Maurice Perez."

I saw a rider lying on the ground. It was a really bad day. I rode over his bike. I reckoned if I'd braked I'd have gone down anyway and landed on top of him, so I might as well go over.

—Francesco Moser

2
Inventing a Race

Le Vélo was new, like the whole sport of cycling. It had begun only in 1892, on December 1. It was distinguished by its green newsprint. Like other sports papers—of which it quickly became the largest—it also covered general news and freely added editorial comment and criticism. That criticism, supporting what turned out to be the winning side in a scandal which brought France close to civil war, led to the rise of a rival, the birth of the Tour de France and the demise of *Le Vélo* itself.

The world's first bike races had been held in 1868 in the Parc de St-Cloud, now a suburb beside Paris's ring-road. The biggest race that day was also won by James Moore, the son of a blacksmith who had moved from eastern England. James was only four when he came to Paris and by 1868 *Jeemie* was more French than English. Among his friends were the sons of the carriage company owner who had the idea of putting pedals on a bicycle. The success that resulted led to abandoning horses and carts and going into bicycle production. He sponsored Moore at St-Cloud and during Paris to Rouen, not just to help a friend but to further his own sales.

Newspapers liked long races because they passed through so many towns and villages. Few people in those days left their village and bicycles were the fastest thing in the world, faster and more reliable than cars. A race from one distant city to another covered a distance greater than most could imagine. Men who spent their days in fields, factories or mines found it easy to imagine the effort, strength and pain that was needed. Create a sensation before the race, trust that people would want to see the heroes pass their homes, and a market was created for sales then and in the future. There was no way to know who the riders were but by buying a paper, and no way to find what had happened, who had won, than to buy another. There was no radio, let alone television.

In May 1891, the *Véloce Cub Bordelais* ran a race from its home town, Bordeaux, to Paris. It was 560 kilometers, not quite the longest feasible distance in France but heading that way. With the support of *Véloce Sport*, the club invited a team from England. The reputation of the English in long-distance racing had been established by the British tradition of promoting long, solo races against the clock. Britain also had a network of town-to-town records of which the longest was from Land's End in the southwest to John o'Groats, the northern tip of mainland Scotland. It was twice the distance of Bordeaux–Paris.

The English, however, had strict rules about amateurism. The Bicycle Union agreed to send a team only if the French matched their rules. The French view was that an amateur could win as much as he liked provided he didn't make a living from it. Even that was generously interpreted: French amateurs were allowed up to 200 francs, a fortune for a manual worker. The English view was that an amateur could win no money at all and had to pay his own expenses. And to ride against a pure professional was out of the question. To do that would turn an amateur into a professional merely by association. And the English weren't going to budge.

The French felt obliged to agree, because they needed the stars. That denied them the best domestic riders and the English consequently took all the leading places. They rode through the night instead of using the camp beds provided by the organizers, who'd been expecting them to take several days instead of just the one that George Mills needed to win.

You'd expect the Bicycle Union to be delighted. But it wasn't. When Mills got home it demanded he prove he had paid his own fare and that he'd received no help from the bike factory for which he worked. Only then would it concede that Mills had triumphed and wasn't a professional.

This wasn't without consequences in France. The historian Fer Schroeders wrote: "The French didn't take kindly to having to respect the law of English amateurism on their own soil because it banned their best professionals. The daily paper, *Le Petit Journal*, therefore decided in June to offer the country's riders a race every bit as crazy: Paris–Brest and back. A race this time reserved exclusively for French riders, a gesture of great patriotism sure to win French hearts."

Paris–Brest–Paris grasped public imagination in a way that Bordeaux–Paris never had. Mills had produced an astonishing effort in Bordeaux–Paris but he and those who finished behind him were English. And they had gone home afterwards. That was of little interest to the French. *Le Vélo* took over all the organization of Bordeaux–Paris and adopted a stricter line with the English. That helped, but the rise of Paris–Brest–Paris and the passions it created—Charles Terront, the winner, was given a box at the Paris opera house and a cream cake was named after the race—overshadowed it.

The weak point of Paris–Brest–Paris was that it was to be run only every ten years, partly to add the allure of the ride of a decade, partly because the promoters thought it too big to organize more frequently. If the people at *Le Vélo* were looking for a way to add Bordeaux–Paris and challenge this new rival, the letter from Roubaix gave them an opening.

Paul Rousseau, to whom the idea was addressed, was the director. His editor was Louis Minart, and it was on Minart's desk that the letter dropped. He read it and he liked it. He would certainly have been impressed by the first prize on offer, because it was what a manual worker earned in five months. But how much did he connive to make sure the letter was written in the first place?

News of a track in Roubaix would have been no surprise to the editor of a sports daily. He would have covered the story, perhaps even gone to Roubaix himself. The historian, Pascal Sergent, says Minart was the two men's "friend." They'd have had no trouble in getting his support, he says.

This is speculation, but the fact that Vienne and Perez suggested their race not on its own merits but as support for Minart's Bordeaux–Paris points either to a lack of confidence unlikely in millionaire industrialists or to some arrangement. Minart knew he didn't have the authority to approve expenditure on such a race and he'd have known, too, that offering it to his directors to support a race they already organized would be an easier path to agreement.

Whatever happened, Minart told Rousseau and Rousseau was so enthusiastic that he told his head of cycling to look into it. In 1900 Victor Breyer was one of six signatories at the founding of the *Union Cycliste Internationale* and became its secretary. He signed on behalf of the USA, although he'd been born neither there nor in France. He was born in Southwold, on the English east coast, because his parents happened to be there in September 1869. He started cycling in 1881, on a high-wheeler, and became a writer in 1886, under the pseudonym "*Veston Gris*" or "gray jacket." It was a reference to the gray uniform worn by his cycling club as it rattled away from the start of its rides in the avenue de la Grande Armée in Paris. The neighbors, having no other name for them, called them the *vestons gris*.

Henri Desgrange made Breyer race director of the Tour de France in 1905 and 1906 but didn't care for his spirited personality and banished him to a desk. He was nevertheless at the top of the Pyrenees in 1910 when the Frenchman, Octave Lapize, shouted "Murderers!" at him, angry at the excess of the new mountain passes the race had been forced to climb.

In 1896, Breyer was still a young man enjoying himself, writing about his hobby. He and his bosses got out their maps and traced a line through St-Germain, Méru, Beauvais, Breteuil, Amiens, Doullens, Hénin-Liétard, Seclin, Lesquin and Hem to Roubaix. And Breyer got on his bike to try it. Metaphorically, anyway. He was stopped by a colleague, Paul Meyan, a tall thin man with sunken cheeks, a beak nose and curly hair. Meyan was founder and editor of France's first motoring paper, *La France Automobile*, in an era when cars were an unreliable, noisy and expensive novelty. He, with glorious company—the Baron de Zuylen de Nyevelt (a prosperous relative of the Rothschild family) and Count Albert de Dion de Malfiance—founded the *Automobile Club de France* over dinner at de Dion's home at 27 quai d'Orsay in Paris.

Meyan had a new 6HP Panhard, a magnificent, gleaming car which now only rich collectors own. He would love to drive Breyer as far as Amiens. And Breyer, who had never been in a car, said he would love to go.

He remembered years later: "I had the luck to ride the first part of my journey in a horseless carriage, thanks to my colleague Paul Meyan, a great pioneer of this new way of travel, who, wanting to try a Panhard

6HP with a steering wheel which he had acquired, offered to drive me to Amiens. The journey, my first in an automobile, was a true delight, notwithstanding my novice's impression of the excessive speed of a vehicle which cruised at around 30 kilometers per hour.

"Stopping only at the places we had planned for riders' controls, at St-Germain (*mais oui!*) [the reason for his exclamation isn't clear], Méru, Beauvais (lunch), Breteuil, Amiens (dinner and sleep), our journey was completed without the slightest snag, a rare performance in those near-prehistoric times. The next morning, Meyan went back to Paris while I continued my journey on my faithful bicycle, which we had brought in the car."

He rode it, one account said, "at the speed of a postman."

"The weather turned to rain, the section between Amiens and Roubaix made worse by atrocious cobbles. It was a true Calvary. I was weak and exhausted, in a pitiful state. It needed the warm welcome of the sportsmen of Roubaix to restore my morale—and to stop my sending a message to Paris advising them against sending riders along the same route."

The French historian Pierre Chany reports Vienne as saying: "One day spectators will have had enough of seeing competitions between riders looking fresh and elegant; they need to be offered the spectacle of roadmen looking exhausted and covered in mud." It sounds like a made-up comment but the prediction, if it was ever made, looked like coming true. There was every chance that riders would reach Roubaix, if they reached it at all, as weak and exhausted as Victor Breyer.

Breyer returned to *Le Vélo*'s office and told his tale. It made the paper's bosses all the keener. They announced their race to the great excitement of cyclists in the north. There, Gaston Nadaud, the director of *Nord Cycliste,* wrote on March 7, 1896: "Great news! A letter that we have received from Mr Maurice Perez and Mr Théodore Vienne, owners and administrators of the Vélodrome of Roubaix, tells of a new sensation: the Paris–Roubaix race. The race will be international, it will cover a course of about 280 kilometers, and it will be held on April 19 next. In sharing with us this news that will make cyclists of our region rejoice, the honorable administrators of Roubaix's track ask our support in making this important race a complete success. Well, of course! You have our immediate support, our good friends!"

Vienne and Perez had suggested May 3. That turned out to be the day of that year's municipal elections. The next choice was April 26, but attention in Roubaix that day would be on the city's horse-racing festival. There would be crowds, the roads would be packed and the vélodrome risked staying half empty. The one date when nothing was happening was April 19.

This dismisses a legend that has established itself as truth. It's clear that Vienne, Perez, Meyan and Breyer went through the calendar looking for dates. Legend says they chose Easter Sunday and that the Church protested. But they didn't choose Easter. They could have but they didn't consider it or thought better of it. They had already looked at other more ordinary weekends.

The Easter Sunday legend has grown to such proportions that Pascal Sergent, the prolific historian of Paris–Roubaix, says: "Sunday April 19, Easter Sunday, was decided on for this first race." Chany added: "The project was condemned wholesale, and Catholic associations put up posters demanding the cancellation of this sacrilegious venture. In response, the two organizers announced that a mass would be said at four in the morning, in the Chapel of Orléans close to the Porte Maillot, where the race would start."

It would be understandable if the Church objected to Easter, but Easter Sunday had been two weeks earlier, on April 5. And if the Church *did* object, and if there were posters demanding its cancellation, it's curious that none has survived in print or on a photograph.

The first Bordeaux–Paris, in 1891, had started on Saturday, May 23. It raced right through Sunday without a break for mass. Riders had reported before dawn for Paris-Rouen. Again, there was no objection to racing on a Sunday or to missing mass. Signing-in at Paris–Roubaix started at 5am and closed at 5:55 for the local riders, who set off at 6, and at 6:20 for the professionals, who left at 6:30.

There can't have been an objection to racing on Easter Sunday because it *wasn't* Easter Sunday.

What seems to have happened is that, whether the Church protested or not, the organizers came up with an early-morning mass to make a good story for the papers. Jean-Paul Delcroix, another historian, confirms the idea was proposed but that the race wasn't on Easter Sunday and that the service never took place. It wasn't until the following year that Paris–Roubaix was held on Easter Sunday—and it was Easter that moved, not the race: Paris–Roubaix was still on its original weekend.

It was on its second running that Paris–Roubaix got its nickname of *La Pascale,* the Easter race.

Amid all this, the organizers set the rules. Any type of bike was permitted and pacers were allowed, on bicycles, tandems and quadruplets; riders were to dismount and sign check sheets at the start, at Beauvais, Amiens, Arras and again at the finish. They were to reach Roubaix within 30 hours or find the judges had left. Once on the track at the finish, the survivors were to ride six laps without their pacers. Those who didn't make it before 7pm were to carry on past the track and report to the Richelieu café. On no condition, the rule sheet insisted menacingly, were riders to abandon their bikes along the way.

The race would start at the Porte de Maillot in Paris, between where the Arc de Triomphe and the tower of La Défense now stand. It was ideal geographically but it was also symbolic. The Porte de Maillot—Paris is surrounded by gates that define the city limits—stands at the end of the beautiful boulevard of the avenue de la Grande Armée. It contained many of the city's best bike shops. A gentlemen's cycling club there met in a hotel with the king of Portugal as its president.

At the suggestion of the *Journal de Roubaix,* which feared local interest would be swamped by stars from elsewhere, riders from Lille and Roubaix could start ahead of the field on condition they accepted prizes in kind and not in cash.

Nobody knows how many entrants Minart hoped for. In fact there were 102, but either the generous prizes weren't generous enough or word had spread of the miseries that Breyer had endured on their behalf. Many didn't turn up. Among them was Henri Desgrange, a talented tricyclist who in his career designed and promoted at tracks in Paris, set a world hour record, and in 1903 founded the Tour de France.

Talent there was in plenty, however. The field included the local star, Maurice Garin already mentioned, the German Josef Fischer, the Dane Charles Meyer who had won Bordeaux–Paris in 1895, and a track specialist from Wales, Arthur Linton, who had an unusual talent not just for speed but for distance. The fact that he was British, given the island's domination in Bordeaux–Paris, gave him more attention than the seven starters from Belgium. France's northern neighbor wasn't yet a challenge in international cycling. One Belgian, however, was Frits Vanderstuyft, whose son Léon broke the world speed record behind a motorbike in 1925 and 1926. Vanderstuyft senior had already ridden Bordeaux–Paris even though he was in his 40s.

Another was Émile van Berendonck, champion of Belgium, founder of *La Vélocipédie Belge*, and subsequently a resident of Paris. He was alone, so far as we know, in competing under a false name. Why his club president suggested he should is a mystery but the organizers accepted him as Eole and that's how he was listed. Such was his talent that the best track stars once refused to race against him in Toulouse.

Van Berendonck never stopped riding a bike, even though he earned a living making automobiles in Paris. He won two French track championships, which in those days were open to foreigners. But in Paris–Roubaix, he didn't finish.

The first thing she'll do tomorrow, just after dawn, is get together all her chickens and cockerels. Rosalie remembers that Bernard Hinault was knocked over by a dog the year he won Paris–Roubaix. It would take only one of them to knock over a rider. "And I'll put our five cows in the shed. The racket of the helicopters drives them crazy," she says.

—*Le Figaro*, 2002, on life beside the route

3
Big Joe, Little Mo

The newspapers picked Fischer to win. That was generous. Not only was he not French but he was the enemy. Germany had besieged Paris and reduced Parisians to eating rats, remember. The Germans killed or wounded 24,000 French soldiers and captured a further 146,000 in just the fighting for Paris. Had the Germans not held back from shelling Paris into submission, there would have been many more than the 47,000 civilian casualties. Among those financially ruined in the siege were the Michaux family who had created the first pedaled bicycles.

The Germans annexed Alasace and Lorraine, eastern territories next to the border, so that to this day the two horizontal arms of the cross of Lorraine remain a symbol of French suffering and liberty. Not for nothing did the Resistance adopt it after Germany invaded again in 1940.

For all that, there was no heckling, no animosity when Fischer arrived at the Porte Maillot. He was 31. He had won Munich-Köburg in 1892, Vienna-Berlin and Moscow-St Petersburg in 1893, Milan-Munich in 1894 and Trieste-Graz-Vienna in 1895. He was also a talented distance rider on the track: he won the German motor-paced championship in 1896 and came fourth in the European championship. He rode all his career for the Diamant bicycle company, although in Paris–Roubaix there was no mention of it on his clothing because there was neither the fashion nor the specialized clothing.

What he looked like on a bike is hard to know. The few pictures are mostly posed. They show his hair neatly parted on the right, slightly receding with a hint of sideburns. A generous mustache spreads across his face and, below it, the sharp and well-trimmed goatee beard of the period. He looks severe, far forward on his bike, his knee almost touching his shallow handlebars, his arms close to vertical. In a rare unposed picture, years later to judge by the more modern bike, the mustache has gone and the beard is an unshaven chin. He stares at the

Josef Fischer: the old enemy, but the French still picked him to win

camera, tired after a race on the track, with the hint of a warm, even sardonic personality.

Reports from the Tour de France, which he rode in 1903 when he was 38, say he had the build of a wrestler. That's not obvious. The pictures show a man of below average height with a developed but not imposing body.

His problem, people said, was that he drank too much. That was why he faded in that first Tour, blaming an upset stomach. It's hard to know what that meant. It didn't mean water. Drinking water is now considered a good thing. But riders drank sparsely until the 1970s. They believed it filled the stomach and stopped their food digesting or, before that, that opening the mouth to drink led to a shortage of breath and therefore dead legs.

It wasn't safe in Fischer's time anyway. The supply in towns was hygienic but the same couldn't be said of rural areas. Countrymen drank wine or beer or cider, because they knew it was clean. In time that led to colossal alcoholism and a ban on drinks advertising in the 1960s which cleared out half the sponsors in the peloton. For riders, alcohol not only wet the whistle but numbed the senses. Riding half-sozzled, as they did much of the time, they suffered less from the broken roads, rotten weather and endless hours in the saddle. When they discovered ether would do the same without making them fall off, they rode with soaked handkerchiefs under their neck and breathed the fumes as they went. Perhaps Fischer was unusually drunk. Or hung over.

Fischer stayed in France until world war one took him back to Germany in 1914. He lived until he was 88, dying in Munich in March, 1953. In the same year, says Franco Cuaz in his biography, Maurice Garin was wandering the northern town of Lens in elderly confusion.

"People often found him from home, walking without knowing where he was going," he wrote. "He asked to be taken to the *commissaire* and they'd lead him to the *commissariat*, the police station. But it was the race commissaire that he was looking for."

The winner of the first Tour de France thought 50 years on that he was still riding it, that he had to sign the control sheet before continuing. He died four years later, in February 1957.

If anyone had picked Garin to win that first Paris–Roubaix then it was through local loyalty. He had talent, he had a bike shop and he belonged to one of the local clubs. He was 25, a good age for a cyclist, but he wasn't yet at his best.

Garin was born Italian, in a hamlet called Chez-les-Garin in the Aoste valley near Arvier, below the Italian side of Mont Blanc. He was related to almost everyone who lived there. Five of the seven families registered there in "*l'an mille huit cent septante et un et le jour quatre mars à huit heures du matin*", as Garin's birth certificate painstakingly spells out in French, were also called Garin. He never spoke Italian to them because Chez-les-Garin was a French-speaking enclave. Or, rather, a patois-speaking enclave since it was unlikely that either Frenchmen or Italians would have understood him.

The story goes that the family sold Garin for a wheel of cheese. It'd be only part of the story. Many people wanted to leave impoverished rural Italy for the opportunity they'd heard awaited in France. That was particularly the case in French-speaking enclaves. Italy worried about just how many wanted to leave and imposed complicated and perhaps expensive conditions. The government's man in Aoste instructed mayors to "categorically refuse, or at any rate to grant with the most diligent precaution, the legal certificate that the law demands to obtain a passport."

In particular, mayors were to beware of unscrupulous touts who "under the pretext of teaching a profession to young children, particularly that of chimney-sweep, try to persuade their parents by promises and unfounded hopes and obtain the children to make a large profit at the expense of their fatigue, their misery and sometimes even their life."

The historian, Alain Rivolla, says the wheel of cheese story "is probably only an anecdote to reinforce the image of a great champion who rose from nothing and overcame numerous difficulties before arriving at the summits, but sadly it's based on an underlying truth.

"Boys were enrolled from the age of six by adult chimney-sweeps who had grown too large to themselves climb up chimneys. They left in the autumn on the roads of France and returned, if all went well, the summer of the following year. Their days were very long, working as many as 14 hours a day, and the working conditions were dreadful, often threatening the lives of these workers who received no direct salary. The employer sent the family a sum of money, equivalent to the price of a calf, on the boy's return home intended for food and clothes. In reality, the boys were often beaten, their masters stole what they received as tips and, in these difficult conditions the little sweeps could die of cold or from a fall in the chimney. They suffered breathing illnesses and became allergic or blind because of the soot.

"Child-employment laws in France in 1874 and 1892 put an end to these dreadful practices for French children but the most determined continued for some years in their dreadful routines by finding children on the other side of the border, in Piedmont." A family which through ignorance or need persisted with the idea could struggle with forms, struggle still more to raise the money, then see everything lost when the mayor turned them down.

Well, difficulties bring solutions, if not always legal ones. Maurice and Maria Garin had nine children. They wanted a better life. Maurice worked where there was work and she, 17 years younger, cleaned and made beds in the nearest hotel. Maurice junior was the oldest of five sons and it's possible he traveled alone to France to avoid detection. Guides were willing to point a way across the mountains and into France at some unsurveyed point. For a price. Barter would have been familiar in a rural economy. The cheese, if there was one, was probably all the family could pay. And Garin, then 14, did indeed become a chimney sweep, as did his brother, Joseph-Isidore.

Life wasn't easy in France, either. The family, which traveled with him or afterward, dispersed and the father returned to the Aoste valley when Joseph-Isidore died north of Paris. Maurice moved several times, to Reims, to Charleroi in Belgium and to Maubeuge, where he bought his first bike. In 1892, as soon as he could, he is said to have taken French nationality at the age of 21. It's therefore as a Frenchman that's he's supposed to have spent his life as a bike-rider. In 2004, however, Garin's biographer, Franco Cuaz, wrote in *La Gazzetta dello Sport* that he had traced Garin's naturalization papers to Châlons-sur-Marne (since renamed Châlons-en-Champagne) and that they were dated 1901, nine years later. He was therefore Italian until then. But, French or Italian, a year later Garin won his first race, Namur–Dinant–Givet.

This, then, was the man who waited in the front row that early Sunday morning, doubtless nervous to find himself beside Fischer, the favorite. The Brasserie de l'Espérance in Paris had stayed open all night to receive the riders and feed them. The first arrived during the previous afternoon, including Garin. He'd trained over the route, he assured his many supporters, and he knew every pothole. The first curious spectators had arrived by 2am at the Café Gillet, on the edge of the Bois de Boulogne, where the riders signed on. Riders who turned up later had trouble pushing their bikes through the crowd. At 4am they could watch the seven riders set off in the race for Roubaix locals. Among them was a professional called Nezeloff who hadn't realized such a race existed but, being 53, decided it perhaps suited him better than riding with the other pros.

Le Journal de Roubaix reported: "The signing-in operation grew complicated because of the number of competitors. The café hall turned into a real paddock where the riders, half-dressed, were examined with curiosity. There were happy shouts everywhere. Among the last to arrive was Garin, who was cheered. Finally, Fischer appeared, the object of curiosity of all, leading him to undress modestly. He gave the impression of pure health and looked a beautiful athlete."

Paris was still in darkness when the list for the main race was complete. Victor Breyer called the riders to the start in the order in which they'd entered. The first hint of light was showing on the horizon. The temperature was three degrees above freezing, gentle weather at that time of the morning and that time of the year. The riders were grateful. The forecast, which came true, was for the weather to stay dry and sunny all day. It had rained for much of the previous week.

A photographer exploded smoking magnesium flashes which blinded the riders and set the spectators coughing. The pictures he took show a field of men almost all with mustaches and pointed beards. All wore ordinary workmen's caps. In the front row stood Fischer, Garin, Meyer, Paul Guignard and Linton.

Two hundred meters away, the Chapelle des Princes d'Orléans was shut. The clerics, Breyer said, weren't prepared to get up at that time of the morning. Which is further confirmation that the Church, if it really had protested, didn't have its heart in it. It'd rather the riders headed for hell than get out of bed to save them. Or, of course, it suggests that Breyer canceled the service himself. But do race officials have the power to tell the world's largest church what to do? Probably there never had been a service. We may never know.

With the field on the line, Paul Rousseau, the director of Le Vélo, stepped forward with a scarf round his neck, lifted a pistol, fired, clicked his stopwatch into movement, and sent the pioneers on their way to Roubaix. Such was the slowness of communication that Journal de Roubaix couldn't get the race into print before the morning of April 21. It made the main headline on the front page—"LA COURSE VÉ-LOCIPÉDIQUE Paris–Roubaix"—but that was a tease because reporting didn't start until partway down the fifth and last column. The start picture wasn't a photograph but a line drawing of a man in a heavy dress coat, his back to the camera, facing a row of riders with trees in the background.

The first Paris–Roubaix got away in a hurry—and it never calmed down. A break had a minute by the time it reached the first checkpoint at St-Germain. They were barely out of the capital but the fact that Linton, Fischer, Meyer, Guignard, Stein, Garin and Sardin had a minute's lead in

32 minutes of racing shows the effort they were putting into it. Paris–Roubaix was three minutes faster than any race that had gone that way before.

But that wasn't enough for Linton. He attacked in the forest which still lies north of the A14 autoroute—not there at the time, of course—and went through Beauvais alone after 86 kilometers at 33 kilometers per hour. Among those pacing him was his younger brother, Tom, aged 19½.

Fischer caught him after a long, hard chase and the two went through the checkpoint together at Breteuil. Fischer was already favorite and Linton was known for his strength and speed over long distances. They knew that a bonus of 150 francs was on offer to the first to reach the esplanade St-Roche in Amiens. Their pacers picked up the pace, so that Garin had lost 5 minutes by Amiens and Meyer had lost 23. The pacers peeled off on the run-in to the sprint, as the rules demanded, and Linton won his money. But while his strength held, his luck didn't. A dog ran into him and he came crashing down at what Pascal Sergent calls an "infernal pace."

Linton took a long time to recover and to mount another bike and he saw Garin ride by before he got going again. Garin reached Doullens and set off up a hill, exposed to the wind, that stretched for 2,500 meters to the hamlet of Beaurepaire. He was still 11 minutes behind the leader and Linton was at 18, still losing time steadily. By Arras, Garin had slipped to 23 minutes, looking tired, and Meyer was gaining on him. The rest were scattered to the northern French wind.

Fischer raced on behind his teams of pacers, avoided a startled horse at Hénin-Liétard and negotiated cows which had spread on to the road a little further on. He rode on to Roubaix through thickening crowds. The idea of a race which finished before their eyes had inflamed public imagination. Thousands cheered as he neared the city. It was the biggest thing villagers had ever seen. Buglers on horseback signaled them to leave the way clear.

"The crowds from Hempempont onwards hindered the riders considerably," the *Journal de Roubaix* reported, "obliging them to ride on the cobbles. The cars, bicycles, tandems and triplets which crowded the road were a serious nuisance."

The paper's specialist colleagues at *Le Nord Cycliste* marveled at just how many people there were, not just beside the road but in the stadium. "The velodrome was black with people," it reported. "People, people everywhere."

Those waiting at the track knew more than those by the road. The organizers had stopped at village post offices to send telegrams giving news to pass on by loudspeaker. Fischer rode into Croix soon after 2:30 and a mass of trumpeters, alerted by the booming, spoke-wheeled cars that preceded him, broke into a fanfare. The pacers who had led him that far peeled off. Fischer turned right on to the track and started the six laps that the rules required. He had ridden for nine and a quarter hours (he finished in 9 hours 17 minutes) at more than 31 kilometers per hour, faster than anyone had dreamed.

A band played the *Marseillaise*. The crowd rose in respect but didn't stay silent: it cheered and men threw their hats into the air. Fischer circuited the track at 31 seconds a lap and reveled in the adulation. He braked at the end of his six laps, dismounted, and accepted a glass of champagne. With that in hand he walked to the register beside the judges' stand, signed his name as first finisher, and disappeared beneath bouquets given by Vienne and Perez, by the city, and by the city's cyclists.

"It wasn't hard," he said. "I rode so that I could take the pavé gently, at my own speed." He stayed by the trackside without going off to change, wandering about, talking, returning to the finish line to see the later finishers.

Clouds were gathering. Charles Meyer arrived 13 minutes later and then, just a lap behind, Maurice Garin, with blood on his shoulder and back. The crowd gasped. They knew he'd crashed but only from the papers did they find out how. Between Ascq and Forest, they discovered, Garin was riding behind his pacing triplet—ridden by two men and a woman—when it collided with a tandem. Garin touched the triplet's wheel and hit the road, passing out. The tandem following them then ran over him, scattering its own riders in turn, its pedal gashing Garin's neck. He was lying there when Meyer passed without a second look. A doctor attended to his injuries by the trackside.

The rain began. Linton entered the wet track 40 minutes after Fischer, exhausted and dispirited by six crashes and a succession of flat tires. Seventeen riders made it to the finish before the track was closed to them. The rest, as instructed, rode on to the Café Richelieu. Accounts of the race say it was in the boulevard de Paris. It's hard to work out where that was. There's no boulevard de Paris listed in Roubaix or neighboring Croix and no café Richelieu. Wherever it was, another 28 riders signed in there before the judges went home. The last—Theron from Antwerp and Dumas from Paris—arrived 30 hours after the start, having stopped for a night's sleep.

Roubaix and the north had never seen anything so thrilling. Back in Paris, folk were much more aloof. *Le Cycle* gave the race just four sentences. What was a race worth if it didn't finish in the capital?

Oh…I never told you about the best amateur. That was Lisseron, who came 13th, 3 hours 40 minutes behind Fischer. Somewhat behind him was a 45-year-old called Mercier. His pluck appealed so much to supporters that they gave him a case of champagne, which they then helped him drink. There was none left by morning.

Paris–Roubaix 1896

Paris Porte de Maillot (rolling start)

Pontoise	23 km
Ennery	25 km
Hérouville	30 km
Vallangoujard	35 km
Amblainville	42 km
Méru	46 km
Corbeil-Cerf	51 km
Ressons-l'Abbaye	55 km
St-Quentin d'Auteil	61 km
Allonne	68 km
Voisinlieu	70 km
Beauvais	72 km
Tillé	76 km
Noirémont	87 km
Froissy	90 km
St-Eusoye	92 km
Breteuil	100 km
Esquennoy	103 km
Flers	113 km
Essertaux	115 km

St-Sauffleu . . . . 120 km
Dury . . . . 126 km
Amiens . . . . 132 km
Villers-Bocage . . . . 144 km
Talmas . . . . 148 km
La Vicogne . . . . 151 km
Beauval . . . . 157 km
Doullens . . . . 163 km
Pommera . . . . 170 km
L'Arbret . . . . 180 km
Beametz-les-Loges . . . . 188 km
Arras . . . . 198 km
Hénin-Liétard . . . . . . 219 km
Courrières . . . . 223 km
Carvin . . . . 227 km
Seclin . . . . 236 km
Wattignies . . . . 240 km
Lesquin . . . . 245 km
Ascq . . . . 250 km
Forest . . . . 254 km
Hem . . . . 256 km
Roubaix . . . . 262 km

My first couple of times on Paris–Roubaix, I had Duclos-Lasalle on the team. For me it was always going to be the biggest one-day race that there is. From the off, the race is important. I did my job and I got in the breakaway. I did about 100 kilometers. I think Duclos-Lasalle and those guys came past me doing about 50 kilometers per hour, and I was doing about 25 kilometers per hour on the cobbles. I literally asked myself: 'What the hell am I doing here, man?'

—Stuart O'Grady, 2008

4
Sticky Endings

Josef Fischer, so far as I know, lived a peaceful and contented life. He came second in Paris–Roubaix in 1900 and 15th in the first Tour de France, in 1903.

Maurice Garin won Paris–Roubaix in 1897 and again in 1898. That first win was far closer than Fischer's pioneering victory, the Dutchman, Mathieu Cordang, right behind him. Pascal Sergent said: "As the two champions appeared they were greeted by a frenzy of excitement and everyone was on their feet to acclaim the two heroes. It was difficult to recognize them.

"Garin was first, followed by the mud-soaked figure of Cordang. Suddenly, to the stupefaction of everyone, Cordang slipped and fell on the vélodrome's cement surface. Garin could not believe his luck. By the time Cordang was back on his bike, he had lost 100 meters. There remained six laps to cover. Two miserable kilometers in which to catch Garin. The crowd held its breath as they watched the incredible pursuit match. The bell rang. One lap, there remained one lap, 333 meters for Garin, who had a lead of 30 meters on the Dutchman.

"A classic victory was within his grasp but he could almost feel his adversary's breath on his neck. Somehow Garin held on to his lead of two meters, two little meters for a legendary victory. The stands exploded and the ovation united the two men. Garin exulted under the cheers of the crowd. Cordang cried bitter tears of disappointment."

Garin won the first Tour de France in 1903 and again in 1904. But then, with many of the other leaders, he was disqualified in a cluster of allegations of cheating. By then he and the Tour were so popular that the *Union Vélocipédique Française* waited until the end of the year

before announcing the bans. Riders had been towed by and even ridden in cars. Riders had scattered nails behind them to delay rivals;
they had poisoned each other or been poisoned by rival fans. Lucien
Petit-Breton said a rider he accused of hanging on to a motorcycle
pulled a gun on him to discourage further accusations. Garin was even

Maurice Garin: local star still to win the first Tour de France

said to have redrawn the rules of cycling by taking a train, a story he
confirmed years afterward to those who cared to listen to his aging
ramblings.

He bought a cycle shop in Châlons-sur-Marne and then, when it failed, a garage in the mining town of Lens. There's still a garage there, although it's not the original, at 116 rue de Lille. In his day three columns supported a long canopy which stuck out towards the road from a square and ugly building. Beneath it stood metal barrels of motor fluid and, in square-cornered capitals with dots above each letter I, "MAURICE GARIN" had been painted by hand on its side. It was wrecked by bombs in 1944.

A fan, a boy at the time, recalled: "I used to meet him and talk to him almost every day because we lived in the same part of town, 200 meters from each other, in Lens. Father Garin, as my father and grandfather used to call him, used to pull out a chair on warm days and sit in front of the office of the service station which he owned, with signs for Antar fuel and oil outside.

"A barber lived in the house which adjoined it and I went there once a month to have a crew-cut, which was the fashion at the time. With my friends—we were all seven to ten years old—we used to get on our single-speed bikes and use pins to put on back numbers that we'd drawn out in pencil. We never missed a chance to ride past Maurice Garin, to show off, in a tight bunch.

"It was strange. Nobody thought to take a picture of me as a little kid in front of the winner of the biggest race in the world. But that's how it was. Maurice Garin wasn't at all an adulated champion and even less a rich champion. He passed his retirement looking after his Antar service station at Lens. I don't remember any special celebration in his honor, no invasions of television teams from France or abroad to interview him before he disappeared in 1957. And the rue de Lille where he lived has never been renamed the rue Maurice Garin."

Garin returned from retirement to ride Paris–Brest–Paris in 1911 and came 10th, almost six hours faster than his victory in 1901. He later promoted a team under his own name, riding in red and white. And then, slowly, he lost his fitness, then his health, and finally his mental balance. He died at 4:10pm on February 19, 1957, a month short of 86 years old. He was taken to the cemetery between Lens and Sallaumines and there he was buried, in lot F3, along with his wives. In his prime, his Latin looks and athletic dash had made him an attractive proposition.

It wasn't until an Italian television crew turned up in 1993 that the cemetery supervisor, a well-built man called Jean-Marie Jasniezicz, realized who was in the cemetery he had been caring for for 15 years. He told me: "Now and again I find flowers here and I don't know who left them. And once a month or so I take a broom to the grave and, out of respect, I sweep round him. But apart from that, he's forgotten, I think."

Forgotten, too, is Arthur Linton, the man who so much wanted to win that first Paris–Roubaix. He and his brothers Sam and Tom were born in Somerset, western England, and crossed the border into south Wales when Tom was three. They joined the Aberdare cycling club. Sam was the best at first, especially over short distances, but Arthur and Tom, said the researcher Stuart Stanton, "went on to gain international fame for their long-distance racing exploits and be-tween them the two brothers broke virtually every cycling record, in Britain and on the Continent, where they were victorious in France and Italy."

Arthur's background is murky and uncertain. It's murky because of his association with a flamboyant trainer and manager called Choppy Warburton. And Warburton is murky because, from the perspective we have now, it looks likely he gave drugs to riders in his care.

Linton rode Bordeaux–Paris shortly after Paris–Roubaix. He won in a draw with the Frenchman, Gaston Rivierre. An account "by one who knows" said: "I saw him at Tours, halfway through the race, at midnight, where he came in with glassy eyes and tottering limbs, and in a high state of nervous excitement. I then heard him swear—a very rare occurrence with him—but after a rest he was off again, though none of us expected he would go very far. At Orléans at five o'clock in the morning, Choppy and I looked after a wreck—a corpse as Choppy called him."

The corpse reached Paris in a daze and then dropped out of races in Paris and in London. Two months later he was dead. His was, accord-ing to the Anti-Doping Forum in Sydney in 2004, the first drugs death in sport. It blamed strychnine, a common drug in distance sports and associated with, among others, the stumbling, glazed-eye victory of Tom Hicks in the Olympic marathon of 1904. The official cause of death, however, was typhoid.

Linton's death shocked Aberdare and his funeral was one of the largest ever in the town. His bicycle was draped in black crepe and pushed behind the cortege by one of his French rivals.

Linton wasn't Warburton's only protégé to die young: the sprinter Jimmy Michael was only 28 in November 1904. And there was also Arthur Linton's brother Tom, who died at 39 in 1914, the cause of death given, like his brother's, as typhoid fever.

Simon Craig, writing in *History Today,* said: "Some have sought to implicate Warburton in their deaths, too, but no direct link seems possible since the trainer himself died of a heart attack in 1897. Even so, it seems highly likely that Warburton did dope his cyclists, and possible that Arthur Linton's death was hastened by damage done to him by drugs administered by Warburton. Yet the symptoms described in the newspapers are consistent with typhoid fever, and we are not entitled to state categorically that drugs played a part. Even with modern drug-testing procedures it is hard to prove guilt or innocence; for an incident more than a century ago, it is impossible."

As for Charles Meyer, the Dane who passed Linton and Garin to come second, he died in 1931, just before his 63rd birthday.

More bizarre was the way Albert Champion died. If you've ever fitted Champion spark plugs to your car, then that's the same man. He won Paris–Roubaix in 1899, a year when the organizers allowed pacing by motorbikes. The sport, remember, was still finding its way and pacers were seen as a way to draw the best out of riders. Bordeaux–Paris had used even cars in 1897, 1898 and 1899 and so in 1899 did Paris–Roubaix.

"On the roads of the north, these noisy cars, high with wooden wheels with their tires nailed in place, raised huge clouds of dust. The drivers, wearing leathers, their eyes protected by huge goggles, were stepping into the unknown. The riders hidden in all this chaos could see absolutely nothing and risked their life at 50 kilometers per hour on a razor's edge. The noise was infernal and the convoy advanced in the stink of exhaust pipes," said Pierre Chany.

The problem was that cars were less reliable than the bicycles that followed. That, and the fact that motorized pacers made the race too similar to Bordeaux–Paris, was why they were dropped in Paris–Roubaix in 1901. But in 1899 they were there and the first to drop out was the favorite, Garin. His car broke down at Vallangoujard, barely out of Paris, and he sat down in despair and disgust as mechanics spent 12 minutes crawling beneath it to bring it back to life.

Pascal Sergent wrote: "He swore he would not restart and, in spite of the pleas of his pacers, he was content to stay seated by the side of the road, waving ironically to the other competitors that he had not long dropped."

One of them was the boyish Champion. He was 21 and already a world record holder. The *New York Times* wrote: "One world's record was broken at Charles River Park [Boston] to-night, it being in the first heat, one mile, of the match race between Albert Champion and 'Major' Taylor, the former covering the mile in 1:29 $^4/_5$ from a flying start. The previous record was 1:30, held by 'Jimmy' Michael."

The paper also reported: "A mile in less than one minute on a bicycle track was set to-day, when bending low over his handle bars in order to make the least possible resistence [*sic*] to the wind, Albert Champion, the great motor cyclist and pace follower, traveled the distance in 58 $^4/_5$ seconds at Charles River Park on his racing motor cycle. It was a hair-raising exhibition of masterly management and of speed. To the spectators it looked as if he was flying through the air rather than following the smooth board surface of the circular track."

Racing behind motorcycles was common on the track, where races went not only fast but far. The attraction for track specialists to try Paris–Roubaix was clear. And for Champion, who excelled at both cycling and motorcycling, the appeal was all the greater.

He passed Garin, to his delight, and told his pacer to pick up speed. The others never saw him again. The only nasty surprise he had was the cobbles, which he'd never ridden before, and he slowed sometimes to walking speed near Arras. It took him two hours to cover the 37 kilometers between Arras and Seclin. His consolation was that those chasing him felt almost as bad and were too far back to gain much time.

Champion was an undisputed winner but it was a Paris–Roubaix *petit cru*. He took 8 hours 22 minutes 53 seconds in good weather, 10 minutes longer than Garin's record time established in rain and wind.

Champion sold bicycles under his name and went to the USA to promote them. He pioneered motor-paced racing in America, returned to France to win the national motor-paced championship there in 1904, then lost interest in cycling. Charles Metz, his business colleague in the USA, had started making motorcycles in 1902. Champion went to work for him, created an improved spark plug and founded a company in Boston, Massachusetts, to make it. He fell out with his backers and started another company in Flint, Michigan. When the backers complained that he was using the same name, he renamed his company AC, after his initials.

A history says: "From its earliest days Champion's objective was to secure and maintain the original-equipment market in the expectation that users who had bought cars fitted with Champion plugs would buy the same brand for replacement.

"Champion had Ford's account for initial equipment from the early 1920s. By 1934 Champion had obtained three other major accounts— of Standard, Humber and Morris. It also supplied plugs, on occasion, to Austin during the late 1930s, and had an increasing amount of trade with the smaller car manufacturers."

Champion was a big name in the industry, therefore, the founder of two of its biggest parts companies. He had an eye for women, who saw him as a good catch. But his marriage foundered when he moved to France and in 1927 he married another girl, described as "in show business". In those days the term carried a connotation of flightiness. She already had, or later acquired, a lover. The lover wanted Champion out of the way and beat up both him and the woman, says Champion's biographer, Peter Nye.

Well, in October 1927 Champion was back in Paris to receive the tributes of the European motor industry, feted in particular for providing the spark plugs that kept Charles Lindbergh in the air during his transatlantic flight earlier that year.

Champion reveled in the applause and adulation of his peers at the Hôtel Meurice. He rose to lead his wife to the dance floor—and dropped dead at her feet, carried off by a heart attack. The company he founded with a borrowed $5,000 in 1905 sold for $750 million in 1989. Champion himself left $15 million. What happened to the lady in show business, I don't know.

The closer we came to the Arenberg forest, the more alone I was. I was already a few minutes behind in the forest. I was going, like, 5 kilometers per hour on the rocks and going bump, bump, bump. It was so bad. I was so upset about how I rode that I stopped at the second feed zone.

—Fabian Cancellara, 2008

5

Nobody Knows the Troubles I Seen

The glory of Paris–Roubaix, hard though it is to imagine now, waned fast. It was just another race and one that ended nowhere convenient. Pacing behind motorcycles and cars made it too like Bordeaux–Paris. It appealed mostly to track riders who had the technique. Some of the road stars persisted—Garin, for instance, trained behind his brother's motor-tricycle for two months—but the rest looked elsewhere. Garin had a local reputation to defend and two wins to celebrate. He carried on.

Only 23 riders entered in 1900 and only 18 of those lined up at the start. Vienne and Perez came close to calling it off. And their mood wasn't helped by the bad temper of Josef Fischer, who punctured six times and then lost his pacers for 20 kilometers after they crashed near Arras. Nor were they encouraged by the ill mood and tantrum of Maurice Garin, furious that he'd been held up by two railway crossings—the fault, he said, of other riders who'd contrived to have the gates closed—and then humiliated by the speed of the winner, Émile Bouhours, who got to Roubaix an hour faster than anyone had done it before, having passed Fischer as he mended yet another tire.

Garin turned up at the velodrome 28 minutes late, in third place. As arranged, his pacing car turned left to park off the track. Garin was supposed to turn right and ride his six laps. But he refused. He rode instead on to the grass of the track center and stopped in a sulk. The crowd cheered and then fell silent, puzzled. Officials ran to tell him to finish the race. He knew the rules. What was going on?

Garin grew more angry. He waved his arms and turned his back and argued and yelled. "I don't care about the six laps," he stormed. "I've got to Roubaix and that's all I care about."

Huge concern. Much embarrassment. The judges compromised. It was clear Garin would still be third even after riding six laps. The next rider, Lucien Itsweire, was too far behind to catch him. They brought the finishers' book to him in the track center and he signed with indifference. He'd ridden 3 kilometers less than everyone else but he got his prize.

News then reached Vienne and Perez of an accident at Croix-de-la-Noailles. Two cars involved in the race had crashed and run into the crowd, injuring 20 people. One of them was the wife of a *député*, a member of parliament. The accident confirmed the end of motorized pacing. The cars had to be dropped to save the riders and their spectators and they had to be dropped to save the race from questions in parliament. Vienne and Perez calculated that little was lost; a motorcycle race on the same course in 1898 proved only 45 minutes faster than Garin on his bike.

But then came fresh trouble.

Le Vélo had a rival. It started in a row which split France over the guilt or innocence of an army officer called Alfred Dreyfus. It sounds insignificant now—except for the unfortunate Dreyfus who was sent to Devil's Island even though he'd done nothing—but it brought France close to civil war. First there was paranoia about the Germans, to whom Dreyfus was said to have sent military secrets. Then there was anti-Semitism. The two brought challenges to the army, which saw itself above criticism, and it spread the charge of anti-Semitism against the Roman Catholic Church, the real power in the land and still more resistant to and resentful of criticism.

Le Vélo mixed sport with political comment. Its editor, Pierre Giffard, thought Dreyfus was innocent. His advertisers, more traditional and already upset by Giffard's high-handed style, were convinced Dreyfus was guilty. And should he happen after all to be innocent, well, it was better he stay in prison than bring dishonor to the army.

Things came to a head. There was a row which peaked, ludicrously, in the president having his hat knocked off. The advertisers despaired and started their own paper, *L'Auto,* to drive Giffard out of business. As editor they appointed a Parisian writer and tricyclist called Henri

Desgrange, the same Desgrange who missed the start of the first Paris–Roubaix. Desgrange agreed to keep the new paper out of politics but his many abilities didn't include originality. If one paper promoted a race, Desgrange ran another. Not something different, as Paris–Roubaix had been, but the same. Desgrange's copying extended to including *Vélo* in the title of his paper, something he had to drop when Giffard sued.

In 1901, Desgrange organized another Paris–Roubaix. It infuriated Giffard, which had been precisely the idea, and Giffard set about promoting his own race on the same day. The affair became an issue in parliament, ending with nothing less than the government of France backing Desgrange.

Le Vélo was furious but powerless. Its days were numbered. Two years later *L'Auto* ran its first Tour de France; the following that it created, and the sales it stole from *Le Vélo,* brought Giffard's end.

A footnote is that in 1904 there was a Paris–Roubaix that never left Paris and indeed never left Roubaix. Just over a month after the gloriously named Hippolyte Aucouturier won the road event before an almost empty stadium—an error meant the gates weren't opened until just before the leaders arrived and the crowd hadn't turned up—the promoters put on a 265-kilometer race on the track. It was as close to the road event as they could manage, the same distance and with intermediate sprints where there would have been controls on the road.

It was immensely dull, of course, but it had a hint of glamor when Émile Pagie, who had married the previous day, turned up in a top hat and tails—*un redingote,* French for a "riding coat". But there was no wedding present: the winner on the track wasn't Pagie but Lucien Petit-Breton, a talented roadman but happier on a track than on cobbles.

On March 31, 1907, Georges Passerieu was not allowed on the track. Or not without a row with the law. He was a heavy-jawed man with deep-set eyes. He was born in England, in London—newspapers referred to him as *le parisien anglais*—although he was French by nationality, through his French father.

By now the dominance of George Mills and Arthur Linton and those both born in Britain and British were over, never to return. Britain confirmed its distance from the continent in general and France in particular by refusing, in the same month as Paris–Roubaix, a tunnel beneath the Channel. The foreign secretary explained: "Public interest leads us to be opposed to this project of a tunnel. Even supposing the military dangers involved were to be amply guarded against, there would exist throughout the country a feeling of insecurity which might lead to a constant demand for increased expenditure, naval and military, and a continual risk of unrest and possibly alarm." Who knows what those French might get up to?

And Britain had lost interest in cycling anyway. Massed races were banned on the road and individual races against the clock, time-trials, were run only at dawn on secret courses with instructions headed "private and confidential." It's doubtful if many in Britain had even heard of Paris–Roubaix, still less cared that a Londoner was about to win.

Passerieu, the Englishman who wasn't, came to Paris–Roubaix with a reputation: he had come second in the previous year's Tour de France. His ride there made him a novelty of the day, a protected rider, a notion of teamwork introduced by the Peugeot team for which he rode.

This isn't without significance. Until then teams had employed a collection of riders expected to look out for themselves. They wore the same colors and drew a check from the same employer but largely they were rivals. The Tour de France archivist, Jacques Augendre, said: "Cycling was considered…a strictly individual sport and the [French] cycling federation was inflexible on the matter."

Peugeot had been making bikes since 1882 and it had used racers to advertise them almost from the start. It had a rival called Alcyon. Each could pay for the best riders around but more was needed, something to give an edge. And that more came from Norbert Peugeot, who became not just the team's owner but its trainer and tactician.

He took on Passerieu because he was fast on the track. He was fast on the track because he rode behind pacers. They took up the speed until he could go no faster. The result was that he could cruise flat out but he didn't have a sprint to see off whoever might remain with him until the end. That was his problem on the road.

Peugeot told his team that Passerieu needed to get into the lead alone. That would get over the sprinting problem; his speed alone would be so great that nobody would stay with him. And nobody would be with him because the rest of the team were to sacrifice their chances to see that he won. And they would know just where they had to do it because Peugeot made them ride the entire route in training.

The word *domestique* for a rider who sells his body to others wasn't coined until decades later. But here in Paris–Roubaix in 1917 the idea of a team with a leader and servants—*domestiques*—was formalized.

As arranged, Passerieu broke clear of the leading group between Arras and Douai and gained two minutes on Eugène Garrigou and Auguste Ringeval. *L'Auto*'s car had reached the finish and spread the news. Passerieu got to the vélodrome in Roubaix in just 45 seconds more than eight hours and prepared for his moment of glory. Bands played and 6,000 people yelled. Passerieu braked for the bend to enter the stadium. And then out from a knot of people at the entrance stepped a policeman.

"I demand you show you have paid your bicycle tax," he insisted. All French cyclists were required to pay three francs. A heated conversation followed. It needed to be: a giant and uncouth Belgian, Cyrille van Hauwaert of the Alcyon team, was at that moment chasing through the streets of Roubaix, less than a minute behind. The policeman relented in the clamor and Passerieu was just short of the finish line when van Hauwaert came on to the track.

Riders were scared of van Hauwaert. At least once he had brought down the whole bunch when he ignored a marshal's directions. In the year he won Paris–Roubaix, he hit a groundsman as he rode on to the track, crashed, climbed back and wobbled to glory.

Van Hauwaert had been a laborer in the fields of Moorslede near Passchendaele, a slaughtering field of the 1914 war. He turned up at La Française in Paris days before Paris–Roubaix, his race clothes in a cardboard case, and asked for a contract. Or gestured, anyway. He spoke little French and could do little but wave a letter of recommendation from Frans Hoflack, La Française's agent in Ypres. In essence, it read: "You won't have heard of the man bearing this letter but sign him and you won't regret it."

Pierre Pierrard, the team manager, opened and read it. He knew Hoflack's name and he knew his company's agents wouldn't send him no-hopers. But even so.... He read as far as "you won't regret it," then looked up again at this man dressed in his country clothes and wearing heavy boots trimmed with metal. Van Hauwaert grinned in encouragement, knowing what the letter said but unable to say much. He spoke in heavily accented Dutch sprinkled with the little French that he knew. Pierrard couldn't understand and van Hauwaert couldn't understand and the commotion grew so great that it brought the firm's boss out of his office. He looked at this jabbering, untidy man, looked at Pierrard and said: "Chuck him out." Van Hauwaert was thrown out on the street along with his cardboard case. He joined Alcyon instead and it cost La Française a lot of money to woo him back.

It's worth remembering that this story has developed with time. Some accounts say the meeting took place in a café and that van Hauwaert rejected La Française and not the other way round. But it's a good tale.

Peugeot worried about this giant Belgian riding for its rival and so in 1908 Norbert Peugeot went further and sent his team to train in the south of France. The man who had created *domestiques* had just created the world's first training camp as well. It should have impressed the other teams but it didn't. They scoffed at Peugeot for wearing out his riders when they needed their energy for races.

The story would end romantically had a Peugeot rider then thumbed his nose at the world by winning Paris–Roubaix. But it didn't happen. Van Hauwaert won the race for Alcyon.

The last rider of any nationality to stand on the podium for half a decade, in 1914, was a wide-faced man with tired-looking eyes and fair hair parted in the center. The fashion for beards and mustaches had passed. His name was Charles Crupelandt and the last section of cobbles before the race reaches the vélodrome in Roubaix is now named after him. It was laid in his honor when the race celebrated its centenary in 1986.

Charles Crupelandt is a small name in Paris–Roubaix. He won in 1912 and then again in 1914, although neither race was an epic. Indeed nothing happened for hours in 1914 and *La Vie au Grand Air*, a sports weekly, regretted: "The victory was, sadly, settled in a sprint and it is a shame that today's roadmen give the impression they think road races are sprint competitions. Old and young alike just wait. Young riders deliberately don't go to the front because they're scared; the older riders watch each other and try not to use too much energy on efforts that may lead to nothing. Where are the Kings of the Road?"

In Roubaix, though, he is big enough to have those cobbles in his honor. Why? Because he was born in the suburb of Wattrelos. And he trained on the track at Roubaix. And he beat the favorite, Gustave Garrigou, a stick-thin Parisian.

That last Paris–Roubaix before the war was on April 12. On June 28, a 19-year-old ran out of the crowd in Sarajevo and shot Archduke Franz Ferdinand. On July 31, France mobilized its army.

Crupelandt was in Berlin at the time, racing on the Olympia track. He got on a train to return to France, stopping at Cologne, Aix, Amsterdam and Brussels, passing himself off as a Dutchman to avoid arrest and spending much of the journey locked in one of the train's lavatories. When he reached France, he joined the 52nd Army Division as a motorcyclist. There, in March 1915, he was awarded the Croix de Guerre after being badly injured in battle. His was one of the first to be given because the Croix de Guerre wasn't initiated until April 2 that year.

In 1917, in circumstances which will always remain unknown—the records have vanished—Crupelandt was jailed. Some say it was for two years but most don't specify. All agree that it was for something minor but nobody knows what. He returned from war a hero and was now disgraced.

But there was more to come. Crupelandt wanted to race again and he asked for a license. This, remember, was a man with the Croix de Guerre, two Paris–Roubaix victories and four stages of the Tour de France. And the UVF refused. He was a convicted felon. And, more than refusing, the UVF banned him for life. Why? Again, we will never know. There were surely bigger crooks in cycling than Crupelandt. And, for all there are stories that riders he had beaten wanted him out of the way, just as much could have been said about many other rivals as well.

Crupelandt *did* race again, but for a pirate organization outside mainstream cycling. He won unrecognized national championships in 1922 and 1923. And then what? Little is known about him after that except that he died in poverty in 1955, blind and with both legs amputated. He lies now in the communal cemetery in Roubaix.

As for others, Cyrille van Hauwaert died, aged 90, in 1974. He had his own bike factory and sponsored a team from 1953 to 1955. There's

Les Woodland

a memorial to him opposite the sports center at Moorslede. Georges Passerieu was gassed in the Battle of the Somme, never recovered and died unknown in 1928 in a hospital for the war-wounded at Sainte-Geneviève-des-Bois.

Missing, too, was the first man to win Paris–Roubaix three times: Oscar Lapize. His friends called him *Frisé*, or Curly, from which we get the English word "frizzy." Everyone, friend or not, respected him for

Octave Lapize: one win is possible, two wins may be luck. But three wins takes class.

winning Paris–Roubaix in 1909, 1910 and 1911. Alphonse Steinès, whose scouting of the Pyrenees led to the Tour's first venture into the high mountains and therefore Lapize's outburst about "murderers", said of him: "You can win one Paris–Roubaix by luck, maybe even twice at the most; but three lucky wins are impossible."

Lapize, a little muscular bundle with a face-wide mustache, the son of a lemonade-maker from Montrouge, had been a professional for just five years when he joined the air force in 1915. He'd won seven classics, three national championships and the Tour de France.

As Sergeant Lapize he became an instructor, then went to the Front in 1917. That summer, he was flying above a French gun battery on the morning of July 14, France's national day, when he saw two German biplanes preparing to attack. He and the Germans scrapped at 4,500 meters until Lapize was struck by a sweep of machine gun fire. He crashed eight kilometers from the trenches and died in hospital.

The air force buried him in a military cemetery and then transferred him at his family's request to Villiers-sur-Marne, where a vélodrome was named after him. He lies there still, above ground in the custom of French cemeteries, in a simple marble tomb. On one side is a picture of him in air force uniform. On top is a crucifix and an inscription which reads "*La Société Historique de Villiers à Octave Lapize 1887-1987*," placed on the centenary of his birth.

The long lists of names on village memorials all over France attest to how many died in France during world war one. Of 8,410,000 men who fought, 1,375,800 died and 4,266,000 were wounded. And that from a population in 1914 of 41,630,000. That's between one in seven and one in eight of everyone in France, or a quarter of the menfolk, dead or injured. Villages died because too few men were left to work the fields and support businesses—or to marry the women. Not until 1950 did the population of France exceed what it had been in 1914.

The "Hell of the North" is how Eugène Christophe described what was left of the devastated areas. "From Doullens onwards," wrote the reporter from *Le Petit Journal* he was accompanying, "the countryside was nothing but desolation. The shattered trees looked vaguely like skeletons, the paths had collapsed and been potholed or torn away by shells. The vegetation, rare, had been replaced by military vehicles in a pitiful state. The houses of villages were no more than bare walls. At their foot, heaps of rubble. Eugène Christophe exclaimed: 'Here, this really is the hell of the North.'"

The hell of the north: Paris–Roubaix is the only race in the world with so strong a trademark.

I think lots of people here in Troisvilles have no idea what Paris–Roubaix coming through here represents. I don't mind at all when people say that Troisvilles is the entry into the hell of the north. The more people talk about this part of the country, the more people will come to visit. There's not much to see apart from the church but you can at least breathe in the smell of the cobbles.

—Françoise, resident of Troisvilles, 2002

6

The Pride of Flanders, the Shame of France

The first Paris–Roubaix when peace returned, but before the Versailles Treaty was signed, was on April 20, 1919. It started after a minute's silence for all the millions of dead and in particular those who'd never again see the peloton. Some races continued through the war. Milan–San Remo, the Tour of Lombardy and the Italian national championship all went on, despite the war. Spain and Holland's championships continued as well, both nations untouched by the conflict. The Ronde van Vlaanderen and Liège–Bastogne–Liège, like Paris–Roubaix, just halted with no clear idea of when they'd restart. People had more important things on their mind.

Cycling had a different face after 1918. The French won 16 of the 19 Paris–Roubaix races from 1896 to 1914 but they won little for the quarter-century following the war. Belgians took 15 of 21 races and many of the supporting places as well.

Why did it happen? It's anybody's guess. Some must have been due to the sheer death toll in France and the need for the remaining sons to work on the farm or in a factory rather than ride a bike. The depth of talent wasn't there.

France's success had probably been due, anyway, to talent mixed with chance. There wasn't much road racing anywhere else. It was banned by law in Holland and by the sport itself in Britain. Spain and Italy were still separated from France by mountains that few chose to cross.

There's an interesting argument that France's decline came from its rush to repair the roads. The repairs in France were either with smoother cobbles or more often with tar. Belgium was in no such hurry and the roads stayed cobbled, as some minor country roads still are to this day. Bad roads restricted travel and Belgians were limited to short journeys suitable for cycling. They stayed used to cobbles and therefore Paris–Roubaix. It's delightful but it sounds tailored to fit the event. Not least because Paris–Roubaix did have cobbles but they weren't a feature of the race as they are now.

The winner of the locals' race back on that first day of Paris–Roubaix was a man named Liseron. From *La Pédale Amusante*, we discover the road surface was good—"true tar for five-sixths of the way," he wrote—although the rest was cobbled, or had tar through which the cobbles showed on worn strips, or had no surface at all. Nevertheless, five-sixths was in good condition.

Roger Lapébie, whose story comes later, said: "The *pavé* then was not as bad as it is now. There were cobbles in all the villages, but we could also take the cycle paths. The problem was that there were punctures. We rode on the main roads, which had smaller cobbles, smoother and more in a mosaic section. There were cycle paths everywhere, so we actually rode very little on the *pavé*."

The more probable explanation lies in the natural cycle of interest and success that nations go through. Belgium was much influenced by Cyrille van Hauwaert's win in 1907. To the Belgians he had succeeded in a foreign land and despite the chauvinism of the French. Rik Vanwalleghem, the Belgian historian, says: "Van Hauwaert became a folk hero who brought in the masses and gave cycling an enormous boost [*zweepslag*] in our country. In 1907 we had barely 125 licensed riders and six or seven tracks. By 1912 the numbers had jumped to more than 4,000 riders and more than 40 tracks."

Flanders was the poorer half of Belgium, dominated by the wealth and power of Brussels and the French-speaking south. It felt itself suppressed and abandoned. Van Hauwaert provided pride. Karel van Wijnendaele, the founder of the Ronde van Vlaanderen, said: "The way he won great victories, abroad and in difficult circumstances, meant a lot to the people of Flanders among whom he was born and grew up. People realized especially that along the beaches of the North Sea there lived a race of people who were healthy and strong. Perhaps not strong in their soul after a hundred years of hard, destructive work but strong in their body and for whom nothing was impossible. Cyrille van Hauwaert was the most typical and symbolic of that race."

The notion of individual sportsmen inspiring a nation is no longer strange to us. In those days it was. In tiny, impoverished Belgium the effect was all the stronger. Belgium had been independent from Holland only 68 years when van Hauwaert won Paris–Roubaix. In all that time, the south had dominated the north, doing its best to suppress the Flemish language—in reality a dialect of Dutch—and culture. It took another two decades before Flemings won the right to be taught, administered and judged in their own language. Van Hauwaert was a public symbol of all that and the history helps explains not only all those black lions on yellow backgrounds—the Flemish flag—you see waved at races but the decades of domination by Belgian riders that followed.

(As a footnote, it's often said that Roger De Vlaeminck, who won the race a record number of times, refused to speak French out of loyalty to his northern roots. The truth is that he used to speak French to journalists from the Belgian south "but the Flemings got cross with me and sent me incendiary letters. It's calmed down since but Tom Boonen is lucky to be able to speak English without annoying anyone.")

Frenchmen therefore no longer had the sweep of the race. Henri Pélissier, who ended up being murdered by his lover, won in 1919. Not without difficulties, though. First he had to gallop after Philippe Thys to stop his winning alone, and then the two of them were forced to stop at a rail crossing while those behind determined that neither should win.

In fact, the bunch didn't catch them. But Honoré Barthélemy did. That infuriated the already irascible Pélissier and he climbed over the crossing barrier and into the train that had stopped across the road. The other two followed, equally with their bikes on one shoulder, barging alarmed and doubtless cross passengers out of the way.

A train is not easy to enter from ground level and it was no simpler to leave on the other side. Encumbered by their bikes, the three climbed and then jumped to the far side of the tracks, scrambled over the other barrier and carried on with the race.

It was the first finish in Barbieux park, the old track having been pillaged by the Germans for the wood and metal that it contained (the

Parc clinic now stands on the site). And he won again in 1921 in front of his brother, Francis, the man who gave Jacques Anquetil his first professional contract.

But otherwise pickings were thin. A Belgian, Paul Deman won in 1920, another Belgian, Bert Dejonghe in 1922, and in 1923 Heiri Suter of Switzerland became the first to win Paris–Roubaix—from a field of 189—and the Ronde van Vlaanderen in the same year. Belgium was devastated: a foreigner had never won the Ronde before. The organizers weren't too happy, either, because the crowd at the finish in Mariakerke was so sparse that ticket sales didn't match the prize list.

Roubaix wasn't too sure, either. The band hadn't considered the possibility of a Swiss coming first and it didn't have the music for the national anthem. Suter had to stand instead for the *Marseillaise*, the French anthem. He'd have laughed: he had laughing eyes in a chubby face that topped a podgy body. Oscar Egg, the greatest Swiss rider of his era, said: "He's a tough guy, the archetype of a modern champion. He doesn't train much but when he does it's fast and I don't know many riders who could stay with him in a sprint."

They did at least have the *Brabançonne*, the Belgian anthem, when Deman won. He was lucky to stand for it: the Germans were about to shoot him as a spy—of which more in a moment. He was a strange man, "the finest stylist I have ever seen" in the words of another great Belgian, Philippe Thys, but impressively shy and tongue-tied. He "expressed himself solely on a bicycle," Pascal Sergent said.

Deman won Paris–Roubaix in 1920 partly through talent but more, as fans and reporters said at the time, through the mishaps of others. It was cold and wet and riders dropped out or simply fell off one after the other. Only four were still in contention at Lens: Henri Pélissier and Honoré Barthélémy of France and Deman and Lucien Buysse of Belgium. And of them, only Deman didn't have a flat tire or other mechanical problems. He rode through Roubaix alone. It wasn't the stuff to warm the shivering crowd.

Even Belgium wasn't sure about him. His gentle, wide-mouthed face smiled slowly and gave him an air of kindness. But he always acted as though really he'd have been happier making carpets, his original job. He seemed as surprised as anyone else to win the amateur Tour of Belgium in 1909 and doubtless wondered what to do with the 41 bicycles he's said to have won in prizes. He was only 19. At 21 he rode his first Tour de France and came 13th.

Then came the war. He was luckier than many—he survived—but only just. The Germans arrested him as a spy, which he was because he rode across Belgium with messages for the intelligence services. Some accounts say, improbably, that they were hidden in a gold tooth. He was caught on the Dutch border on his 15th or 25th mission—accounts vary—and jailed in Leuven. He was due to be shot when he was saved by the Armistice.

Deman did well on a bike but he could have done better without persistent stomach problems. He was a regular in Roubaix and the consulting rooms of Professor Fauverghe, a specialist in gastric complaints. He had an operation on a gastric hernia after the war.

After Deman came the generation who'd grown up inspired by Cyrille van Hauwaert. A boy old enough to ride a bike in 1907 was too young to fight in the war but just the age to race after it. And one after another they came to Paris and won in Roubaix: Bert Dejonghe in 1922, Jules van Hevel in 1924, Félix Sellier in 1925, Julien Delbecque in 1926, Georges Ronsse in 1927, Charles Meunier in 1929, Julien Vervaecke in 1930, Gaston Rebry in 1931, Romain Gijssels in 1932, Sylvain Maes in 1933, Gaston Rebry again in 1934 and 1935, Lucien Storme in 1938, Émile Masson Jr in 1939.

From the end of the second world war until the last of Roger De Vlaeminck's wins in 1977, Belgians won 26 races in 35 years. Although not without incident, naturally.

Things started turning sour in 1927. One of the dullest ever races started without many of the stars; the Doullens hill which had always been decisive played no role at all; the race just rode on and on and on with nothing happening. The pace picked up only at the end and two men rode clear of the 16 leaders in the streets of Roubaix. Georges Ronsse, a Belgian who the following year became world champion, entered the finish straight with Joseph Curtel, a lesser known rider from Marseille, on the Mediterranean coast.

Reports say they rode an epic sprint along the avenue des Villars and the crowd rose to its feet as Curtel won by just the width of a tire. Hats were thrown into the air, arms waved, voices raised. A band broke out with the *Marseillaise*. A Frenchman had won for the first time in six years. Curtel was carried on the shoulders of his fans. Before he could accept his bouquet Ronsse snatched it away from the hands of the young girl about to present it.

"You don't steal my Paris–Roubaix like that," he shouted. He turned to the judges and warned them what he'd do if he met them on the street.

And then the judges gave it to Ronsse.

"There was almost a riot," Pascal Sergent records. Fights broke out between Frenchmen and Belgians in the crowd and for a while it looked as though the judges would have to flee. They'd been swayed, bribed or perhaps even threatened by Pierre Pierrard, the man who had failed to sign Cyrille van Hauwaert and who was now Ronsse's manager at Automoto. Pierrard was therefore also a candidate for lynching.

But who was right—the French spectators or the Belgians?

Ludo Feuillet—a former medical student who'll play a bigger part in Paris–Roubaix shortly—was there to look after his Alcyon riders. He made a neutral witness. "I was right opposite André Trialoux, the judge on the finish line," he said. "I had a perfect view of the peloton and I could see that the Alcyon riders were surrounded and didn't stand a chance. So I concentrated on the leaders and I saw with my own eyes that Ronsse crossed the line with just a quarter of a wheel before Curtel, who'd been coming up fast from behind. I heard the *Marseillaise* and I assumed that Trialoux had seen Curtel as the winner. There were so many people on the road that I had trouble getting across, but when I got there I asked the judge: 'Did Curtel win, then?'

"He said: 'No, it was Ronsse.'"

So what had happened? It took a while to find out but it seems one of Curtel's supporters had been sure his man had won and had run to tell the conductor of the band beside the road. It was the tradition then to play the national anthem the moment the winner was known and the band opened up with the *Marseillaise*. That had convinced French supporters they'd seen something that hadn't happened. Only when films were developed and photographs printed was it clear that Trialoux was right, that Ronsse on the left of the road had beaten Curtel.

One reason Pierrard was assumed to have swayed the judge was that it was then well known among the knowledgeable that big teams had power in and outside races. It was enough that in 1930 Henri

Desgrange decided that he would rather pay all the riders himself during the Tour de France than put up with the scheming of professional teams and, especially, their officials. When he heard what happened in Paris–Roubaix that same year, he'd have felt justified. And he'd have heard a lot about it because the race director was a young Jacques Goddet, who succeeded him as organizer of the Tour.

It was a classic example of the power of a big team overwhelming that of a smaller one. On one side was Julien Vervaecke, another Belgian, and Feuillet's Alcyon team. On the other was Jean-Baptiste Maréchal, a stubborn Parisian who had started as a boxer and then turned to cycling and landed a semi-professional contract in the little Colin team from the Eiffel Tower area of Paris. There was loyalty in that—Colin had built his first bike—but word said he'd held out for too much from bigger teams.

This was the last Paris–Roubaix to be ridden on fixed wheels. The big guy and the little guy had been away for 60 kilometers by the time they reached Roubaix. Vervaecke was from northern Belgium. His manager, Feuillet, was French and it was in French that he shouted "Don't work!" to his rider. Maréchal understood but realized he'd be better off doing all the work himself, coming second to Vervaecke, than refusing and being caught by the chasers. There was just the chance that he could win—who knew if Vervaecke would fade or fall?—but even second place would be a huge step for a minnow riding as an independent, the halfway stage between amateur and professional.

Feuillet, whom riders called *Père*, was not a man to challenge. His control of the Alcyon team was such that he once drove one of his own riders off the road so that his favorite would win. And yet Vervaecke disobeyed him. He zigged to one side and on to the sidewalk, passing Maréchal by 15 meters. Maréchal was tired from his long solo effort but he was even more angry to see the man he had been taking to the finish, a far more talented rider, just profit from his effort and ride off ungratefully. On aching legs he fought back and caught him again.

The two came together at a point the road narrowed. The surface was poor, the two men were tired and each was angry with the other. That one touched the other surprised nobody. Riders don't usually fall when they touch elbows, *frotter* as cyclists call it but Vervaecke did. He toppled into a ditch.

The fall caused more dismay than hurt and he got back on the road, remounted and began to chase. Maréchal had turned 20 only two months earlier. He had been a cyclist for only four years, taking his first license on the day after his 16th birthday. His world looked like being made and he wasn't going to give up now. He had only a few lengths' lead but he increased it until by the length of the avenue des Villas he had won by 24 seconds.

To the crowd, to the waiting officials who knew nothing of what had happened, there was no contest. Maréchal had won. But then they were confronted by the angry, demonstrative and powerful figure of "Père" Feuillet. He made a menacing figure with his slicked dark hair parted in the middle, a wide mustache and gold-rimmed spectacles.

At this point, it's worth pointing out that race organizers in those days carried as much weight as judges, that the race was organized by *L'Auto* and directed by its leading cycling writer, that Alcyon was a big rich team that could buy advertising in *L'Auto*, which always needed the money, and that *L'Auto*'s other race, the Tour de France, had chosen Alcyon to make the supposedly anonymous yellow bikes that all Tour riders would now ride. There were at least two business links between Alcyon and *L'Auto* but none at all with Colin.

It may be that Feuillet didn't need to point out any of that. His presence would have said it for him. But there was more. As the Franco-American journalist René de Latour said: "Cycling as a pastime was popular, and accordingly the French and Italian cycle firms were big and powerful. To get the top market it was necessary to get into the public eye, and the best way to do that was for their riders to win the big classic events and so obtain enormous space in the newspapers. At Easter, the cycle magnates used to await the result of Paris–Roubaix with anxiety. To win it was a godsend, to lose it was sometimes a disaster."

Alcyon may have had the contract to supply Desgrange's yellow bikes but the Alcyon name wasn't on them and under Desgrange's new Tour de France of national teams, there would be no Alcyon team in the Tour. The publicity event of the season had been denied to Alcyon and to all other sponsors. If Vervaecke didn't win Paris–Roubaix, Alcyon's factory at Courbevoie, near Paris, would be in trouble. Paris–Roubaix now is 10 weeks or more into the professional season. Then it was the second race of the French year, after the Critérium International.

To all this background, Feuillet insisted his rider had been knocked off and that Maréchal, who had done it, shouldn't have won. He was joined by Vervaecke, who was sharing his protests between the judges and Maréchal. The story for the Belgian supporters who joined in grew until it appeared Maréchal had deliberately pushed their man into a ditch of water.

"It's scandalous," Maréchal retaliated. "Our elbows barely touched. He fell off because he was tired. I've fallen victim to *la taule*." Such was Feuillet's discipline in the Alcyon team that riders referred to it commonly as *la taule*, or prison.

Of the few who'd seen the incident, none thought Maréchal had done anything deliberate. Romain Bellenger, who had just stopped racing to take up team management, said: "Our car was alongside the two of them. Maréchal was riding on the cobbles and he too jumped on to the stretch at the side. As he tried to reestablish his balance he touched elbows with Vervaecke, who fell. It was as simple as that."

Feuillet couldn't go as far as say that Vervaecke had been deliberately pushed off. It's hard now to know just what he *did* argue, except that his man's chances had been harmed and that he ought to be compensated. And for that to happen, Maréchal had to be demoted to second place. To which, after a lot of heat and noise, the judges agreed.

But that wasn't the end of it. Maréchal pointed out that if he was guilty then he should have been disqualified, not demoted. That was what the rules said. But he wasn't disqualified and therefore he must be innocent. And therefore the protest should be thrown out.

But he got nowhere. The big guns were all on Alcyon's side.

Was Maréchal just lucky on the day but denied at the end? Seemingly not. He had talent. Fifteen days later he won Paris–Tours and, still just 20, he was the only Frenchman that year to ride the Giro d'Italia. When he retired he managed regional teams in the Tour de France in 1950 and 1951 and owned a driving school in the crowded 15th *arrondissement* of the Paris left bank. He died, aged 83, two days before Christmas in 1993 and he's buried in the cemetery at Maules, in the Yvelines region. He was bitter to the end of his life about the injustice he suffered on April 20, 1930.

Vervaecke came to an equally unhappy if more sudden end. In May 1940 he was shot by soldiers of the British Middlesex Regiment after refusing to give them his house and furniture. His body wasn't found until weeks later, on the Belgian-French border. His death is one more shrouded story of war.

They say there's going to be mud on the cobbles tomorrow. That's good. For a lightweight like me, it's an advantage. The more slippery it is, the more the big, strong riders, the Big Bears on the cobbles, slide about. And the longer that I can ride with them.

—Frank Vandenbroucke, 2004

7

Riders and Judges at War

Roger Lapébie was never a man to leave officials untroubled. The whole Belgian team walked out of the Tour de France in 1937 after he clung to cars in the mountains and, in their view, was only lightly penalized. Such was the contempt in which he was held that his handlebars were sawn partway through before a stage in the mountains and he found out only when they snapped before the start. The French and Belgian teams had shared the same hotel.

In 1934 Lapébie was disqualified after winning Paris–Roubaix. He was 23 and riding in the blue, white and red of national champion. He, his fellow Frenchman René Le Grevès, and the Belgians Gaston Rebry and Jean Wouters, were clear of the field on the last stretch of cobbles. Grevès broke his handlebars and then, 10 kilometers from the finish, Lapébie flatted.

"My car could have changed the wheel," he said in 1992, "but it had got stuck behind the other race vehicles. I had got rid of my spare tire and pump because we were so close to the finish. I rode on the rim, then found a woman's bike in a ditch and jumped on that. A little further on I saw a man's racing bike in the ditch, got on that, caught the other three with 500 meters to the line, got away from then and won."

French fans were delighted, except perhaps the man whose bike had been stolen and the woman who had to walk home. But the jubilation didn't last long. The rules said he couldn't change bikes. Officials had fixed seals to all the bikes the previous night to be sure it didn't happen. Rebry's manager protested, dragging Lapébie's illegal bike with him, and the judges had no choice: the Frenchman was disqualified.

"They had played the *Marseillaise* for me and then I was disqualified," he said. "I was disqualified without even being credited with second place."

"I knew the risk I was taking in changing bikes," Lapébie told the Tour de France archivist, Jacques Augendre. "I made the right decision and, so far as I'm concerned, I won Paris–Roubaix."

He never lost interest in cycling. He was a regular guest on the podium of the Tour de France when it finished in Bordeaux, near his home in Bayonne. For a while he was the oldest surviving winner of the Tour—his victory in 1937 was the first on derailleur gears—and, with Gino Bartali, the only surviving winner from before world war two. He drove guests "at frightening speeds" during Paris–Nice.

The writer Gordon Daniels said of him: "Cycling was the passion of Roger Lapébie's life. A vegetarian from 1933, uncommon for a professional racing cyclist, he continued riding long into retirement and until shortly before his death. His death in October 1996 marked the end of an era."

The rule forbidding bike changes was changed the year after Lapébie's disqualification. But craftier riders had already found a way round it. Félix Sellier, for instance. Sellier was the seventh of 13 children and worked as a miner in a poor region of Belgium. Like many, he escaped poverty by riding a bike and he came to notice when he won the independent, or semi-professional, Tour of Belgium in 1919. He was a rugged man with a wide mouth, sunken cheeks and a mop of hair brushed back without a parting.

The year he won Paris–Roubaix—1925—there was just one serious break all day. Sellier was in it and so was Jules van Hevel, who'd won the previous year and expected to win again. Apart from those two, the rest were mostly regional riders. And suddenly Sellier was pushing a gear as large as a motor-pace follower's on the track. His legs turned just once for everyone else's twice.

It was a trick that Sellier had pulled in Paris-Brussels the previous year but only rumor could say how he did it. The idea, of course, was to reach the finish with a sprinting gear the others couldn't match. But the rules forbade bike changes and Sellier couldn't have ridden the whole way on a gear so large. So how? Well, the secret escaped. Sellier had started on a single gear the same size as everyone else's.

But nearing the end of Paris-Brussels and then Paris–Roubaix he had feigned a puncture. While appearing to replace the tire, he took a 14-tooth sprocket—the smallest available—from a string round his neck and screwed that on instead. It made an already excellent sprinter unbeatable in the sprint.

But the effort shattered him and he passed out after the finish. He came round to the sound of the *Brabançonne*.

Incidentally, if you recall the case of poor Jean Maréchal, the case was reversed in 1936. It was a tricky year for Europe. There was civil war in Spain and the Nazis had control of Germany. France was still a democracy but the left-wing alliance which looked like winning the election was welcomed by many—it introduced paid vacations and a 40-hour working week—but portrayed by right-wingers as communist. Their views were sharpened by strikes which broke out across the country.

Nobody knows if that influenced the judges. Probably not, not directly, although nations unite when threatened. It would have showed solidarity when the nation needed it. And when the Belgian, Romain Maes, pulled up alongside the Frenchman, Georges Speicher, on the cinder running track of the horse-racing circuit, the judges gave the race nevertheless to the Frenchman.

Wishful thinking had had its way. Speicher was a better sprinter than Maes and the third man in the group, Gaston Rebry. Speicher was national champion and he had won the Tour de France and world championship in 1933. So he was the winner. Except that he wasn't, as photos prove. Maes, on the right of the pair, had won by a few centimeters.

And the crowd knew it. Belgians, who'd come to see Paris–Roubaix as an early-season championship, rose and shouted and waved. Even some of the French protested. But, as Pascal Sergent says: "This time injustice favored a Frenchman. People remembered the episodes which involved Curtel in 1927, Maréchal in 1930 and Lapébie in 1934."

The world was indeed changing. In Paris–Roubaix it was low key, in that an Italian won for the first time in 1937. Greater men had failed—Costante Girardengo and Alfredo Binda included—but a barely known rider of 23 succeeded. To be fair, Jules Rossi was more French than Italian. His parents died when he was six and he moved with the rest of the family to France. They settled in Nogent-sur-Marne, a sub-urb now of eastern Paris.

He grew up there and in 1928, when he was 14, he started cycling. He made a fast impression and joined, or was invited to join, the Vélo Club de Levallois on the other side of the city. There was no club more powerful in France than the Levallois. It was run by the flamboyant Paul Ruinart, a man who created many champions but had a leaning towards *les mignons,* the better-looking ones. He made no secret of it,

Émile Masson: a Belgian bringing pride back to Flanders

said the French historian Pierre Chany, who knew him. Rossi, with his long, slender face and brown eyes, may have appealed.

Ruinart took Rossi's talent and perfected it so that he produced a string of impressive victories almost from the day he joined. Ludo Feuillet took him into the Alcyon team in 1934. Three years later Rossi rode to the front of Paris–Roubaix in rain along with a group of

Dutch-speaking Belgians. Feeling isolated, he attacked to rid himself of as many as he could. He was helped by discord among the Belgians, as much rivals to each other as they were to Rossi.

If there was one thing Rossi could do, it was ride fast. He went to the front and, in the way Eddy Merckx was to ride four decades later, he raised the pace until nobody could stay on his wheel. He won by several lengths with the rest of the breakaway arriving as individuals.

And then, with two more races, world war two. The winner in 1939, Émile Masson, was called into the army just three days after his victory. He was taken prisoner by the Germans on May 12, 1940, and spent five years to the day in internment. On his release he emptied a kilo can of coffee to rescue an abandoned Belgian flag and take it back home. "He couldn't bear to see it left on enemy territory," wrote a historian, "so he decided to empty a can of coffee to carry it home." He lived until January, 2011, when he died aged 95.

The winner in 1938 was less fortunate. Lucien Storme, another Belgian, was a round-faced man with fair, wavy hair. He won despite a flat tire in the last eight kilometers. The following year he won a stage of the Tour de France before abandoning three days later. He joined either the Resistance or the ordinary army after Belgium was invaded in 1940—accounts vary—and he was taken prisoner by the Germans in December 1942. They sent him to a camp in Siegburg, near Cologne. He survived there until April 10, 1945, the day that American soldiers liberated the prison—and shot him by mistake. He was 28.

France declared war against Germany on September 3, 1939. Nothing happened for months. Enemy troops stared at each other across the Rhine, neither side hiding, neither opening fire for fear of provoking a battle. It was the *drôle de guerre*, the phony war. And then in 1940 Hitler's Panzers bypassed the Maginot Line by attacking through the Ardennes—considered unbreachable by France's elderly generals—and then in a separate movement south through the main part of Belgium. The two armies encircled the Allies on the Channel coast near Dunkirk, forcing thousands to abandon their equipment and stand in the sea until rescued.

"You don't win a war by retreating," growled Winston Churchill.

The Germans reached Roubaix on May 24, 1940. Henri Desgrange died three months later, on August 16. His successor at both *L'Auto* and its races was Jacques Goddet, its chief reporter since 1936. Goddet and his brother, Maurice, owned many of *L'Auto*'s shares, inherited from their father, Victor, the financial director.

Goddet insisted until his death in December 2000 that he did nothing to further the German cause and that he turned down German requests to organize the Tour de France during the Occupation. His role at *L'Auto* in those years is ambivalent. He supported Philippe Pétain, the first-war general who sought an armistice with Germany and became its puppet leader. But that was no different from many other Frenchmen, the majority when the German invasion turned to a rout, who saw Pétain as giving France as honorable a route as it could hope out of the carnage.

More questionable is that *L'Auto* under Goddet's editorship printed news contributed by and favorable to the Germans. Decades afterward Goddet insisted that he had little choice, that his hands were tied because his brother had sold his shares to a German syndicate close to the Nazis. The argument didn't sound convincing even at the time and only tributes paid to him by associates swayed the decision at a postwar inquiry.

Goddet's autobiography, *L'Équipée Belle,* a play on words which can mean both "the wonderful escapade" or "*L'Équipe* is wonderful"— *L'Équipe* being the paper he founded as a successor to *L'Auto*—mentions denying the Germans only the Tour de France. It says nothing of Paris–Roubaix. But *L'Auto*, under Desgrange, *did* try to promote Paris–Roubaix in 1940.

The Germans refused to let it finish in Roubaix because its army was on the Belgian border. Goddet suggested running the race in the opposite direction, south to Paris, but that died when the *préfet* in the Somme—the President's representative—refused to have the race on his territory. The compromise was to run a token event between Le Mans and Paris. It was known formally as the Trophée Duralumin, after a make of bikes, but the banner across the start made it clear that this was Paris–Roubaix. There were 63 riders, including two foreigners. The race finished on the Parc des Princes velodrome in western Paris, which *L'Auto* rented, and it was won by Joseph Soffietti.

There were two more nominal Paris–Roubaix races after the invasion, approved and probably even desired by the Germans.

France by then was divided into zones. The two best known were the Occupied area to the north of a roughly central line and the so-called Vichy area, known for the small spa town chosen for its administration, in the south. But there were other areas, and Roubaix was in one that also administered Belgium. It was the price it paid for being part of a conurbation that spread both sides of the border. Travel between zones was difficult and ruled out the traditional route for Paris–Roubaix. So the 1941 and 1942 races were between Paris and Reims, won by Jules Rossi and Émile Idée.

The risk of invasion from North Africa, which the Allies had invaded, led Hitler to occupy all France in 1942. The significance of administrative borders declined and Paris–Roubaix could again be run on its original course. If the other wartime races had some justification, organizing Paris–Roubaix in its traditional form, with German permission and cooperation, didn't fit Jacques Goddet's insistence that he did nothing to placate the Nazis. The records of both *L'Auto* and the Tour de France and other races have all disappeared. They were put in a truck and driven south on roads clogged with refugees when the only sane thing to many seemed to be to flee the invasion. The refugees and other travelers were strafed by the Luftwaffe and the truck was never seen again. But *L'Auto's* keenness to resurrect the race despite the Occupation is made clear by Pascal Sergent.

"[Goddet did not] stop preparing for the organization of an eventual Paris–Roubaix. After lots of difficulties and problems, he was finally recompensed when the authorities came to the offices of *L'Auto*. The event could be reborn after three interrupted years."

The Germans had promised to find Goddet all he needed—food, bikes, transport and fuel—if he'd re-run the Tour de France. It's hard to think they didn't make the same offer for Paris–Roubaix. And yet Goddet makes no mention of it.

Well, these were other times and it's dangerous to judge by hindsight. There was no sign in 1943 that the Occupation would ever end. Pierre Chany, who knew the man well, said: "I'm not going to judge Jacques Goddet. It's not my role. I haven't the right. But to those who want to blacken his name, I'd say this: Jacques Goddet never sold anyone.

Jacques Goddet, during the war, ran his business, kept the shop open. In a way, yes, he was passive towards the Occupiers. But no more than 98 per cent of Frenchmen in 1940."

It's never scared me. In the end it's just a race. You have to just keep on riding and hope that nothing happens to you. It's a race of natural selection: the strong and the lucky survive.

—Michele Bartoli, 2004

8

And Why Does Any of This Matter?

The Tour de France and therefore the empire that owned Paris–Roubaix was formed by one war and died in another. *L'Auto* was founded by businessmen who believed Dreyfus had sold secrets to the Germans. The row reeked of resentment that France had lost the Franco-Prussian war. After another and bigger war, France wasn't in a rush in 1945 to give national institutions back to their pre-war owners. The Vichy government under Pétain had suspended the Republic and peace gave a chance to start again. Renault was confiscated because it had built trucks for the *Wehrmacht*. Newspapers tainted by German propaganda were shut down. *L'Auto*'s doors were literally nailed closed.

Goddet was alarmed. He no longer had a newspaper, he no longer had his bike races, and to some he was a collaborator. It was he who owned the Vélodrome d'Hiver, the indoor track near the Eiffel Tower, and who had handed the Germans its keys so they could cram thousands of Jews inside before deporting them to their death. It is another episode which Goddet dismisses.

When Goddet could see as everyone else could see that the Germans had lost the war, he became a *résistant de la dernière heure*—someone who joined the Resistance when victory was assured. He helped assault a Paris ministry occupied by the Germans. He could now claim Resistance credentials, he could insist the Germans gave him no choice but print their news, and he could say he had an active resistant on the paper's management. Stories that he encouraged his printers to turn out Resistance pamphlets and Charles de Gaulle's speeches were untrue but he wasn't going to deny them.

The government let him start another paper on condition it wasn't called *L'Auto*. But it didn't give him the bike races. The Communist paper, *L'Humanité*, wanted to run those through its magazines, *Sports* and *Miroir Sprint*. Charles De Gaulle wouldn't countenance a French monument falling to communists and so Goddet got the Tour for lack of competition. He had saved Paris–Roubaix and the Tour de France— but only just. From now on they would be run by his new newspaper, *L'Équipe*.

By 1944 the Germans had been pushed out of France. The D-Day forces had landed in Normandy and Paris had been liberated in August that year by the French army in the west of the city and the Americans in the east. The rest of the country had been cleared by Operation Dragoon, the invasion of the Mediterranean beaches that has dropped out of popular history. Goddet, resistant the final hour, considered it safe to run Paris–Roubaix. It bumped over roads that hadn't been mended since the invasion of 1940.

Nobody pretended that the riders were fit. Food was hard to get and time for training even more so. Bike tires were just about impossible to get and the small supply passed, as did much else, on the black market. Riders raced for prizes in kind, sold them for cash and bought food and bike gear. But the race was back on the road, won unexpectedly by a 23-year-old Belgian, Maurice de Simpelaere.

The man the Belgians hoped would win, their teenage national champion, Rik van Steenbergen, pulled out after a crash. So, too, although it didn't seem significant at the time, did a little man from Brittany who looked like Mr Punch. Jean Robic tumbled at the feeding area in Amiens. He got back on his bike and managed to finish the race although with a headache.

Transport was short and Robic returned to Paris in a truck. He vomited so much that he passed out. Helpers called a doctor, who diagnosed a broken skull. Robic spent three months in hospital and thereafter wore a leather crash helmet. It gave him the nickname of Leather Head.

And then came the farce of 1949, with two winners who'd taken two different routes. One—the first chronologically—was the Frenchman,

André Mahé. The other, a few minutes later, was Serse Coppi, brother of the more spectacular Fausto Coppi. And what happened? Well the two Italians were close and Fausto was aware that his brother suffered in his shadow. With the two of them in the break, Fausto gave Serse a push and let him ride clear. He wanted him to win.

Behind them, Mahé watched and waited. When nothing else happened, he started to chase. He reached the leaders and then attacked again, taking with him Jésus "Jacques" Moujica and a Belgian, Frans Leenen. From those three, Mahé attacked again and gained a short lead.

André Mahé: note the bottle with a cork stopper.

Mahé remembered: "At the entrance to the velodrome, there were crowds everywhere, blocking the way. I looked around for where to go and I was directed round the outside wall of the track, to where the team cars had to park. It wasn't like nowadays, when there's television and everything. Then it was more chaotic and the whole road was blocked."

A report in *Sport Digest* explained what happened next:

"At the crossroads [at the entrance to the track] there was an advance party of several dusty cars. Someone in one of them shouted: 'Three riders away: Leenen of Belgium and Moujica and Mahé of France.'

"Someone on the sidewalk asked if he knew what had happened to Fausto Coppi and Rik van Steenbergen, the two big favorites. But by that time the car had turned to the right, just as it was supposed to. Suddenly we saw the three champions whom the roads had turned into Negros. A big red Hotchkiss car, from *L'Équipe,* was following them fairly close and gave the impression of pushing them along at 50 kilometers per hour. Then right behind was the blue Jeep from *France-Soir.*

"The policemen were saying to themselves 'Riders straight on, vehicles to the right.' But hell! They all got there at the same time. They made one sign to block the route and simultaneously to divert the cars. The Breton, Mahé, thought that signal was for him. With Leenen and Moujica behind him, he turned sharply in the wrong direction."

There was pandemonium with officials, marshals and policemen trying to correct the mistake while at the same time dealing with a bunch of 50 bearing down on them.

Mahé said: "People said I should have known the way into the track. But how do you know a thing like that at the end of Paris–Roubaix, when you've raced all day over roads like that? A gendarme signaled the way to go and that's the way I went. It was a journalist on a motorbike who managed to get up to me. He was shouting 'Not that way! Not that way!' And I turned round in the road."

The journalist was Albert De Wetter of *L'Équipe,* who went on to become assistant director of Bordeaux–Paris.

Moujica started to turn in the narrow space. He fell and snapped a pedal. Mahé and Leenen left him and rode back the way they'd come, the wall of the grandstand beside them. On the other side, thousands of spectators had heard the leaders were about to enter the track and had begun to wonder where they were. Leenen's chain came off.

Mahé said: "I saw a gateway that went into the track, a gateway for journalists. And that's the way I went, except that it came out on the other side of the track from the proper entrance."

He outsprinted Leenen and won Paris–Roubaix. And then the bunch rode into the track and Serse Coppi won the sprint. The judge,

Henri Boudard, had either seen nothing odd in Mahé's entry into the track or was too confused to know what to do. Mahé was named the winner and he set off on his lap of honor with his bouquet across his handlebars. He had won the dull-sounding Rizla Cigarette Paper Trophy.

Not knowing what was about to happen, he rode off the track and looked for the showers. When he came out he heard Fausto had told Serse to protest. Mahé may have crossed the line first but he hadn't ridden the whole course. The next morning *L'Équipe* printed the result on the first page without Mahé in it. The headline said "Mahé, first after riding 200 meters too far, disqualified."

I met Mahé, a weary, shuffling man, at his home in Choisy-la-Bac. He'd been born a year after the Armistice was signed in a forest clearing two kilometers away near Compiègne. These days it's where Paris–Roubaix starts, although he never went to watch that or any other race unless invited. He was still bitter, disillusioned, about the way he'd been treated.

"Even the French federation interrogated me. I felt like a condemned man. They seemed to take the view that I had cheated somehow. I ended up having to justify myself, even though all I'd done was follow the way I'd been directed."

Five days later the *Fédération Française de Cyclisme* overturned the result and reinstated him and kept Leenen as second. "It couldn't be otherwise," said its president, Achille Joinard. But that wasn't going to please the Italians and they complained to the UCI. The world governing body struggled for four months and in August said the only thing to do was cancel the race and its two results. It would decide what to do in November when it met in Zürich.

Serse's brother, Fausto, told French journalists at the Vélodrome d'Hiver in Paris that he wouldn't ride Paris–Roubaix the next year if Mahé was given the win. "I want before anything else that Serse is given his victory," he said. There were just days before the UCI had to decide. The threat was clear.

The issue took on a hidden dimension because there was an election coming up for the UCI's presidency. Joinard wanted—and got—the job but to do it he had to keep all the member nations sweet. And that included the Italians, the loudest voice in the assembly. The next two

strongest were France and Belgium, but the Belgians had sided with
Italy. Why it sided with Italy wasn't clear but rumor said it was to spite
the ghost of Henri Desgrange, whom everyone knew had been the
kingmaker in international cycling.

"The UCI just did what Desgrange told it," was how Pierre Chany
put it. Desgrange was dead but Goddet could be warned.

Joinard couldn't solve the problem *and* further his ambitions. And
that upset France, which accused him of treachery for soft-pedaling
Mahé's cause. The UCI met again that November and maintained the
race but gave victory to both. "Thank heavens there's another Paris–
Roubaix in four months," one of the delegates said.

Mahé died, still unhappy, in October 2010. "Coppi wanted his
brother to have a big victory," he said. "He was a great champion, Coppi, but to do what he did, to protest like that to get a victory for his
brother, that wasn't dignified for a champion. That was below him. A
champion like that should never have stooped that low. I never spoke
to him about it. Never did. Why should I? For me, I had won Paris–
Roubaix."

*Serse Coppi (second from left): his brother stooped too low to contrive
his win, said André Mahé*

It's the true definition of hell. It's highly dangerous, above all in the first kilometer when you hit it flat out at 60 kilometers per hour. It's incredible. The bike goes everywhere. It's a real spectacle but I don't know if that's a good enough reason to subject us to it.

—Filippo Pozzato on the Fôret d'Arenberg, 2006

9

Neither From Paris Nor To Roubaix

It was called Paris–Roubaix but in fact it wasn't. It finished not in Roubaix but in Croix, because that's where the track was. It's a small distinction but Paris–Roubaix didn't finish in Roubaix until 1919. Why? Because the original track was a ruin by the end of world war one in 1918. The Germans took the metal to reinforce their trenches and townspeople took the wood to burn in place of coal. It stood, sad and crumbling, until it was taken to bits and finally demolished in 1924. It marked the end of what Victor Breyer called "the most interesting attempt at sporting decentralization which has ever been attempted since cycling became the most popular French sport," meaning that it shifted the sport out of the capital and into the provinces.

By the next century, the sport would be trying to decentralize itself further from continental Europe and shift out into the world.

Roubaix did have another track: the Parc Municipal, created in 1914 where the current track now stands. The spirit of the time was to encourage activity in the fresh air, especially for children. In Roubaix, this was the initiative of a pioneering doctor named Dupré. Every Thursday afternoon and daily during school holidays he encouraged Roubaix's children to play there. The concern after the war was to bring an end to tuberculosis, for which the general cure was to isolate patients in clean surroundings. If that worked for those who had caught it, who was to say it wouldn't work as well to prevent it? And so Roubaix gained a tuberculosis treatment center in June 1921.

In October 1927 the idea grew into an open-air school, the *École de Plein Air*. The primitive showers that now greet riders at the end of Paris–Roubaix are in one of the surviving buildings from that period.

For the moment, though, the finish the organizers chose wasn't on a track at all. That—the one we know now—had yet to be built. The replacement finish was behind the dairy on the avenue de Jussieu and then at another stadium, the Stade Jean-Dubrulle. From then on it moved every few years, from 1922 until the start of world war two in the avenue des Villas—renamed the avenue Gustave-Delory in 1937 in honor of the man elected mayor of Roubaix, the first socialist mayor in France, in the year that Paris–Roubaix started—with exceptions in 1929 (the Stade Amédée-Prouvost in neighboring Wattrelos), and in 1935 and 1936 (the Flandres horse-racing track in Marcq-en-Barul).

The move to Marcq-en-Barul was the result of a tiff between the race and the city. *L'Auto* shrugged and took its race elsewhere. It persisted, though, in calling it Paris–Roubaix. That caused great offense among Roubaix's powerful and on April 3, 1935, the mayor sent a lawyer, André Dautriche, to *L'Auto*'s office in the rue de Faubourg-Montmartre in Paris to protest. To finish anywhere but Roubaix was unthinkable and to keep the original name was a confidence trick. Either *L'Auto* found a finish in Roubaix or it must change the name. If not…if not…

Well, if not, what? Dautriche was powerless. He came home empty-handed and *L'Auto* moved to the horse track. Why? Because it could charge for tickets in a stadium but not if the race finished on the road. Nevertheless, it moved back to the avenue Gustave-Delory in 1937, 1938 and 1939.

Change was still happening at the open-air center, the Pont Rouge. The most significant for cycling was the work that started in 1936 to build a cycling track with a running track within it.

It took another war to move the finish to the new track, situated between the avenue Roger Salengro and the avenue des Parc des Sports, which finally acquired a grandstand. Only three times has it left there—1986, 1987 and 1988—to finish in the avenue des Nations-Unies, to satisfy La Redoute, the mail-order company which sponsored the race and had its offices there. It was an unpopular choice and the finish moved back to the track.

From the second year until 1923 Paris–Roubaix was run on Easter Sunday. For 63 years the race stuck to largely the same route. There were minor changes such as in 1906 when the race skipped Hénin-Liétard–Carvin because miners were on strike after Europe's worst pit disaster killed 1,099. The colliers and those who sympathized were angry and the organizers feared for the riders' safety. Spectators gave the riders such a welcome in Douai that the race went that way for the next three years.

In principle the route otherwise stayed the same, passing through Pontoise, Beauvais, Amiens, Doullens, Arras and Hénin-Liétard before Roubaix.

The roads through St-Paul-sur-Ternoise and Béthune were introduced in 1919 because the original route was impassable because of war damage. Otherwise for years the race was a straight run up the main highway to Lille and Roubaix. Even so, riders used tires of 350 or 400 grams rather than the 300 of today's Tour de France. Partly that was because tires weren't as good then but it was also, as Roger Lapébie explained, because "It was important not to have too high pressure in the tires. You got fewer punctures that way. Sometimes we used wooden rims because they are more supple than aluminum."

In 1898 the mayor of Paris refused to let the race start in the capital, complaining that it added to the city's traffic problems. The same administrators in 1903 refused to allow the Tour de France to start or end in Paris.

The start of Paris–Roubaix moved to Chatou, then in 1900 to St-Germain before returning for the last time to the Porte Maillot in 1901. After then it moved several more times before settling on its present site, the town of Compiègne. Given that the race the "Hell of the North" was created by world war one, Compiègne has that unintended significance: it was in the railway car in a forest clearing there that Germany signed the Armistice.

Starting City by Year

1896–97	Porte Maillot
1898–99	Chatou
1900	St-Germain
1901	Porte Maillot
1902–13	Chatou

Les Woodland

1914	Suresnes
1919–28	Suresnes
1920–22	Chatou
1923–28	Le Vésinet
1929–37	Porte Maillot
1938	Argenteuil
1939	Porte Maillot
1943–65	St-Denis
1966–76	Chantilly
1977–	Compiègne

The greatest change was in the nature of the race. And it came because of the second war. France was among the winning nations but it was bankrupt. It had been bombed, invaded and fought over by both sides. The Allies alone bombed 1,570 French towns or cities. The raids killed 68,778, destroyed 432,000 buildings and wrecked 890,000 houses. The Germans had taken half the country's meat, a fifth of its vegetables and even a fifth of the champagne. Two million soldiers were held in German prison camps, hostages to force the French to cooperate in sending Frenchmen for compulsory war service in factories in Germany. Their absence depopulated the countryside and crippled farms.

The government's reconstruction ministry calculated that if the whole country spent not a centime on anything but getting the country back to how it was, it would still take three years. There would have been little hope for the country, or for others in Europe, were it not for Marshall Aid. In return for commercial concessions—Coca-Cola secured its place in France thanks to Marshall Aid and despite the resistance of wine makers—the USA gave France $2.3 billion over three years. It started three decades referred to in France as *les trente glorieuses*. The French standard of living rose to one of the world's best by 1975, with high wages and consumption and widespread social benefits.

A consequence was that the roads were improved. At first there were 60 kilometers of cobbles, of which two thirds led into Roubaix. André Mahé said: "After the war, of course, the roads were all bad. There were cobbles from the moment you left Paris. There'd be stretches of surfaced roads and often there'd be a cycle path or a sidewalk and sometimes a thin stretch of something smoother. But you never knew where was best to ride and you were for ever switching about. You could jump your bike up on to a pavement but that got harder the more tired you got. Then you'd get your front wheel up but not your back wheel. That happened to me. And then you'd go sprawling, of course, and you could bring other riders down. Or they'd fall off and bring you down with them.

"And the cycle paths were often just compressed cinders, which got soft in the rain and got churned up by so many riders using them and then you got stuck and you lost your balance. And come what may, you got covered in coal dust and other muck."

Surfacing began just before world war two, starting with Forest-sur-Marque and Hem in 1939. Nobody minded. Roads were for year-long travel and not only was Paris–Roubaix insignificant by comparison but, the roads all over France being bad, bad roads didn't create the race's reputation. Instead, Paris–Roubaix was known as an attacking race, because it was flat, because riders had limited gears, and because it was shorter than other classics.

France's rise to prosperity accelerated events, however. By 1955 there were just 31 kilometers of cobbles and by 1965 only 22. A forecast by the roads ministry in Paris that there would be no cobbles left on the route within six years looked like coming true. Mayors who administered areas along Paris–Roubaix didn't care to have their poverty displayed on cinema newsreels and on fledgling television.

"Why do you bring us this terrible publicity?" one frustrated and hard-up mayor asked the organizers in 1952—before surfacing the road to stop Paris–Roubaix coming that way again.

The speed rose and a different race evolved. Rik van Steenbergen broke the speed record in 1948 and Peter Post of Holland did it again in 1964. His 45.1 kilometers per hour is unlikely ever to be broken.

Alarms sounded. Albert Bouvet, the race director, said: "If things don't change, we'll soon be calling it Paris–Valenciennes," referring to a flat race on good roads that ended in a mass sprint. Jacques Goddet forecast the future could be a circuit three times through the Forest of Arenberg before finishing in Roubaix or elsewhere. And people grew nostalgic for the bad old days. What was the point of Paris–Roubaix if it swept north on fine, restored highways? They remembered how the world champion, Georges Ronsse, had crashed a hundred meters from the finish in 1929 and run to the line with his bike on his shoulder.

The first changes came in 1955, when the course grew 20 kilometers longer to take in more cobbles. But local pride struck: no sooner had the race ridden the cobbles of Moncheaux and Caouin and the pas Roland than the tar-spreaders arrived to wipe them out.

Things became so serious that the start was moved to Chantilly so that the race could explore further to the east. That took the race through Hornaing, Ferrain, Rieulay and Flines-les-Raches. The cobbled stretches now came to 40 kilometers. And still the search went on. And still the resistance retaliated.

Alain Bernard, now himself mayor of a northern commune—Bouvines—is president of *Les Amis de Paris–Roubaix*, an enthusiasts' group which finds and maintains cobbles. "In the 1970s, the race only had to go through a village for the mayor to order the road to be surfaced," he says. "Pierre Mauroy, when he was mayor of Lille, said he wanted nothing to do with the race and that he'd do nothing to help it."

Of the 250 *Amis de Paris–Roubaix*, the most prominent was Jean Stablinski—not because the old world champion was any grander than members such as Pino Cerami, Gilbert Duclos-Lasalle, Marc Madiot, Alain Bondue and the former Tour de France organizer, Jean-Marie Leblanc, but because he discovered the 2,400 meters of the Fôret d'Arenberg.

It has scared riders ever since.

It is the trademark of any self-respecting journalist that he should get names wrong. Or make them up. *Cycling* in the 1960s received a news agency report from a world championship which lacked a rider's first name. Since nobody had heard of this rider, and since he was Belgian, there seemed no harm in calling him Willi Merckx. But how French reporters managed to turn Edward Stablewski into Jean Stablinski is known only to them. Stablewski's family was one of many to emigrate from Poland to the mines of northern France between the wars. They came in such numbers that the population of Wallers grew from 4,018 in 1901 to 6,392 in 1931 despite the slaughter of villagers in world war one.

Edward's new name stuck and in 1948 he took French nationality and, officially, the name Jean Stablinski. He never won Paris–Roubaix, although he rode it 11 times and finished twice in the first 10.

"It came just a bit too early in the season for me," he said. "I can say that three times I could have won but, the rest of the time, the whole bunch would have had to fall off to let it happen."

Stablinski's career was closing when Albert Bouvet, a new course director following Jacques Goddet's orders, enlisted Stablinski to help find cobbles. Stablinski found the sectors at Famars and at St-Saulve. But above all he recalled the Fôret d'Arenberg that now follows them. The road had been laid to link the villages of Wallers, Hasnon and St-Amand-les-Eaux. It fell into disuse when other roads were properly surfaced and eventually only miners used it to get to their pits. A few amateur races had been along it but nothing else.

The first Paris–Roubaix to go that way was in 1968. Miners stood at its entrance in their overalls and helmets.

"If I remember right, I was the third to reach the road at the end and Walter Godefroot was the first," Stablinski said five years before his death in 2007. Godefroot attacked to be among the leaders at the railway crossing that marks its entrance. "It lay before me," the Belgian said, "strange and disturbing, and there were immense puddles of water. I attacked through it, but I was sick to my stomach. If I had hit one hole or disjointed pavé, it would have meant an immediate accident, flat, or broken wheel."

Stablinski was scared of going into the showers at the end of the race. "They called me every name under sun," he said.

The mine beneath the Arenberg road closed in 1989. Stablinski used to work down there because his father had died when he was eight and he had to help his mother, a seamstress, support the family. As a boy he earned money playing the accordion at weddings and village dances.

"It wasn't a time of opulence," he said drily.

He always claimed he was the only rider to have passed both along and beneath the Arenberg track. He heaved coal 300 meters below ground in gallery 262 for nine months until his talent on a bike allowed him to escape. "I didn't work down there long enough to suffer," he said, "but I can tell you that I'd rather ride up the Galibier than be a *galibot* [apprentice] down a mine."

Bouvet was delighted by Stablinski's find and started searching the countryside for other paths that didn't show on maps. Alain Bernard, too. He was riding his bike one Sunday in 1980 when, on a whim, he turned off the road to see what was there. He discovered the Carrefour de l'Arbre—Tree Junction. It is now the last bad stretch of cobbles before the finish.

The Carrefour de l'Arbre is where Marc Madiot, now a team manager known as "1,000 Volts" because of his temperament, made his winning moves in 1985 and 1991. When the photographer asked to take his picture there years afterward, he declined. He was too superstitious, he said. He preferred not to "go back to the places of my previous exploits."

One morning Alain Bernard took a break from his marketing job at La Redoute, the mail-order company in Roubaix which sponsored the race, and drove me out there. The road is flat, broken and splashed with mud from the fields on each side. The landscape is broken by plantations of tall, spindly trees destined to become telegraph poles or parts of furniture assembly kits but, apart from them, there's no life. There's no real crossroads and, since the few trees are temporary and commercial, the junction shares its name with the squat and ugly bar that sits there.

It has two stories, the windows of the upper projecting into the steep, tiled roof. The name of the place is printed in large red capitals screwed to the left of the shuttered entrance and again at the crest of the roof in black tiles set among the red.

There must have been passing trade there for centuries. The first drinks license goes back to 1274. But times changed. "Until the race came this way", Bernard said, "it was only open one day a year. In France, a bar has to open one day a year to keep its license. That's all it did, one day a year, because it's out in the middle of nowhere and nobody went there to drink any more. With the fame that the race brought it, it's now open all year and a busy restaurant as well."

It may have done too good a trade on race days. The crowd who'd stood on the corner outside the bar was so rowdy in 2009 that the mayor threatened to ban the race from passing. Spectators had spat on the riders, thrown beer on them and stumbled into their path. Belgians had run out to hinder those who were chasing their favorites.

Crops were trampled and mounds of litter left, including long lines of beer cans and plastic glasses.

The mayor's discontent was in contrast to colleagues elsewhere. For attitudes changed and, instead of wishing the race would stay away or resurfacing the roads that it took, in the last decade they have smiled on it. Why? It's hard to say why any attitude changes. New minds arrive, fresh eyes watch the situation. The crowds along the road become not a problem but an answer—people who book hotel rooms, tank up their cars, eat in restaurants and buy beer in bars, food in

Alain Bernard, the devil behind the Carrefour de l'Arbre cobbles

shops. Trade in a poor area is to be welcomed, not discouraged. And it becomes clear from television coverage that the farm tracks of Paris–Roubaix are merely that—farm tracks and not the everyday roads of the region.

Beside the road or in front of a TV could be an industrialist looking for a site for a new factory. If he went away from the Nord not liking it, well, too bad. But better that people come and see for themselves and be won over. All publicity is good.

"That's why the mayors call us to tell us they've found somewhere new," Bernard says. "It brings the race and the publicity to their commune. We no longer go out looking for *pavé* because there's so little left that it's no longer worth our time. We may go down a track to see what's there, out of curiosity, but that's all. It's the mayors now who do the looking.

"Whereas once cobbles were the last thing a village wanted to boast, they're now back in fashion. They give village centres a rustic look and the mayors see them as a great way to keep traffic speeds down. So the old craft of *paveur*, which was just about dead, is back in demand. And what better way to give the new *paveurs* experience than by putting them to work on Paris–Roubaix, restoring what the Nord now realizes is its heritage?"

The race that began the change was in 1948. Nobody had much thought about the cobbles then but Rik van Steenbergen's average 43.612 kilometers per hour was faster even than Jules Rossi's 42.092 kilometers per hour in Paris–Tours. And Paris–Tours has fewer climbs and doesn't have the cobbles either.

It was van Steenbergen's first ride in Paris–Roubaix but he was no outsider. He'd been Belgium's national champion in 1943 and 1945 and he'd won the Ronde van Vlaanderen in 1944 and 1946. Three riders were clear of Paris–Roubaix as it went through Hem, six kilometers from the finish. The French champion Émile Idée, the balding Italian Fiorenzo Magni and the Belgian, Adolf Verschuren, thought the winner would come from their trio. But then van Steenbergen started to chase, taking three more with him. They took advantage of the driver of a film truck who kept just ahead of them, but not so far that the riders couldn't profit from his slipstream.

The groups came together in the streets of Roubaix. Idée didn't have a sprint to beat van Steenbergen and he tried to ride him off his wheel. After a leg-tearing effort, he looked round. He had got rid of the rest but van Steenbergen was still there. Idée was beaten. He flopped to the grass of the track center and confessed: "I didn't have the strength to get away from him and what can anyone do against him in a sprint? Wherever I ride, there's always a *flahute* to steal my victory." *Flahute* is an argot word in southern Belgium, at the same time insulting and flattering, to describe a strong Belgian from the north. It carries respect but also connotations of big legs and a small brain.

Van Steenbergen's record speed in his debut Paris–Roubaix was helped by a violent tailwind for the whole distance. And he lost the record anyway in 1955, when Jacques Dupont pushed Paris–Tours to 43.666 kilometers per hour in 1955.

What Paris–Roubaix needed, after that and then the farcical outcome of 1949 and its two winners, was something to remember. And it got it.

Fausto Coppi came to Paris–Roubaix on Sunday, April 9, 1950, to take revenge. He had ridden against van Steenbergen on the track and

Fausto Coppi (right), erratically brilliant on the road, troubled by life off the road

on the road. If there weren't any mountains, which remained a mystery to van Steenbergen until the day he stopped racing, it wasn't obvious which of the two was better. And Coppi was cross that van Steenbergen had beaten in him in the Flèche Wallonne after, he said, tucking in behind cars to catch him.

Coppi was in turmoil. His home life had turned sour. He was embroiled with a woman his biographer, Jean-Paul Ollivier, described as "strikingly beautiful with thick chestnut hair divided into enormous plaits." Rumors were already spreading and distaste in Catholic Italy grew to such a point that in time even the Pope was provoked to comment. On the bike, Coppi could do everything and then find it wasn't enough. In 1949 he became the first to win the Tour de France and Giro d'Italia in the same year. Yet Ollivier recalls Italian newspapers predicting that "Coppi will win no races in 1950 because he will pay for the efforts that he produced last year."

Another reporter wrote "His style is not suited to the character of the great international classics," adding as a sweep-all that he wasn't much good in Italian races either—he had just lost Milan–San Remo because of a flat tire and despite chasing back to the leaders—and not even the Tour de France, despite having just won it.

Ollivier wrote: "Cut to the quick by this, he paid a visit to his team manager, Tragella, to draw up a plan of battle for the most prestigious of all road races: Paris–Roubaix. Pinella de Grandi, his mechanic, built up a machine specially adapted to the cobblestones of the north. He would be surrounded by solid and faithful men, his *gregari*, Conte, Pasquini, Crippa, Milano, Carrea and Serse Coppi."

He was cautious and inquiring at the start, asking where the cycle path was best at Wattignies and about the weather. He sought every way to make it tough. "If the race isn't hard," he said, "there'll be 40 of us together at Roubaix and I'll get beaten by van Steenbergen and the Italian journalists will criticize me again. My fellow countrymen are never happy."

Journalists asked what he intended to do about it. He looked at them and said: "If I get the chance, I'll shake up the bunch on the hill at Doullens. It's got to be a hard race, you understand?"

The weather was bad. Three domestiques rode beside and in front of Coppi to provide a human shield against the wind. The race referees kept their car windows closed against the rain and didn't see the domestiques giving Coppi pushes.

The attack at Doullens didn't come from Coppi but from Jacques Moujica, one of the riders sent the wrong way at the end of the previous year's race. Coppi was on him straight away. He passed him and reached the top alone. Five riders got up to him—but not van Steenbergen. Not immediately, anyway. He had to chase with 15 others.

The race approached Arras along the route des Mousquetaires and riders slowed slightly to grab the cloth bags of food held out by helpers. It takes only a few seconds to string the satchel's strap over one shoulder and to empty it into the pockets at the back of a rider's jersey. But it's a skilful thing to do while riding in a bunch of a hundred or more riders, all of whom are also concentrating on more than keeping a straight line.

Coppi had already taken food from his teammates. He didn't need more at Arras. He took the lead casually as the field reached the feeding station and then, breaching the ethics of cycling, accelerated through. A little Frenchman, Maurice Diot, had been leading the race and he managed to stay with Coppi as he came by. He even had the strength and speed to share the pace-making. It was then that his team manager, a taciturn farmer and former rider called Antonin Magne who addressed all his riders as *vous* rather than the informal *tu*, made a tactical mistake. He ordered Diot to stop helping the Italian. His reasoning was that Coppi would grow tired without Diot's help, that he would slow down and that Diot's team leader, van Steenbergen would catch him.

Coppi didn't understand. He had a deal that the two would reach Roubaix together and ride a straight sprint. He pulled over for Diot to take his turn at the front, then looked back when the Frenchman didn't oblige.

Diot shook his head. "Not allowed to," he shouted. "Van Steenbergen's chasing."

Coppi, dismayed, rode to the edge of the road and left Diot in the wind. He attacked once to see if the Frenchman could stay on his wheel—he had no intention of dragging Diot to Roubaix only to be beaten by fresher legs—and then attacked a second time. Diot faltered. When Coppi surged again, Diot crumpled. Coppi cleared off alone for the 45 kilometers that remained.

He rode, Ollivier wrote, with "a style and in a purity rarely to be equaled, continuing to increase his advantage. During the last hour of the race he struggled alone on sidewalks which were hardly ridable and on the terrible roads, and yet he covered more than 41 kilometers in one hour."

He finished with enough of a lead that the others didn't even see him in the showers. By the time they got there after milling in the track center, he had left for a track race elsewhere. He had come in almost three minutes before Diot and five and a half before Magni. And van Steenbergen, for whom Diot had been ordered to surrender his chances, trailed in nine minutes later.

Diot got off his bike and shouted: "I've won Paris–Roubaix!"

"And Coppi?" the journalists asked.

"Oh, he doesn't count," Diot laughed. "He's in a class of his own."

Coppi came back in 1952 a saddened man. He'd come close to abandoning cycling after his brother, Serse, crashed and died in the Giro del Piemonte the previous summer. *The Bicycle*, rival to *Cycling* in Britain, reported: "The two brothers were still with the main bunch a kilometer from the end of the 272-kilometer race. Fausto was not moving with his usual smoothness and Serse was by his side with words of encouragement.

"Then three riders crashed, but only one did not continue the race—Serse Coppi. He was actually able to ride to the hotel, and it was not believed that he was seriously hurt. But he was subsequently taken to hospital, where concussion of the brain was diagnosed. He died in Fausto's arms before an operation could be performed."

His wheels had caught in the tracks of the Turin tramway.

It was a bad year for Fausto, not just his brother's death but a broken collarbone in Milan–Turin. His absence and his drop in talent were matched by the fall in value of his vélodrome contracts. To get those and his criterium engagements back to value, he had to perform well from the start of the season. Which meant Paris–Roubaix.

Cycling reported: "It was a classic duel—van Steenbergen, the brawny Belgian sprinter, versus Fausto Coppi, the fragile thoroughbred from Italy. Two years earlier, Coppi had risen to new heights with his lone epic after dropping breakaway partner Maurice Diot. Now history was repeating itself.

"Coppi was in the lead and again he had a sprinter for company—van Steenbergen. Repeatedly Coppi attacked in an effort to rid himself of the Belgian. Van Steenbergen had made a huge effort to get across to Coppi and admitted to dying a thousand deaths as he hung on to the *campionissimo*'s wheel.

"The hill at Hem was Coppi's last chance. He threw everything into an attack, but although van Steenbergen was suffering mightily he somehow he stayed in contact. The sprint was a foregone conclusion—van Steenbergen won easily." Well, maybe not so easily because he had no sooner got off his bike than he sank to the grass, drank a bottle of milk for want of anything better and vomited immediately.

He said: "If he'd attacked just once more, I'd have had it."

Reporters passed the confession on to Coppi. His permanently sad face teased a little smile. "If I'd had just a drop of strength left, I'd have attacked him. I kept trying and he kept getting back up to me. I thought he was fresher than he was."

Van Steenbergen recounted: "On the hill at Hem, I gave everything I had in my guts. Coppi was going so fast that I thought any moment I was going to sit up. And then to my relief he slowed down. If he'd done

Rik van Steenbergen: from Paris-Roubaix to a sex fantasy

it again, I could have cracked and then everyone would have said that I accepted Coppi's superiority, and I'd never do that."

Van Steenbergen raced from 1942 until 1966. Even he could never say how many races he had won, let alone ridden. A conservative estimate says he won 52 as an amateur and 270 as a professional, including

around 40 in stage races, and 40 six-days on the track. Wilder esti-
mates say he won 1,000, although that's 41 for every year of his career.
By comparison, Eddy Merckx won 525 races, amateur and professional, and Roger De Vlaeminck 509.

He was famous for riding wherever there was money, sometimes
accepting contracts for two races in the same day. *Cycling* recalled: "He
made several appearances at London's Herne Hill track. One London
promoter was shocked when van Steenbergen demanded his appear-
ance money in cash minutes before a meeting was due to start. With
the crowd growing impatient, the promoter had to do a fast whip-
round of the turnstiles and empty his own wallet before van Steenbergen consented to take to the track."

His enthusiasm for money was such that in 1968 he acted in a sex
film, *Pandore* (also known as *L'amour aux bougies*), in which he con-
vincingly played a thick-waisted Greek sailor for whom the heroine
had a fondness.

Van Steenbergen's reputation was already then at its deepest. He fell
into bad company, as he put it himself, when he found himself with
nothing to do outside cycling. He became a heavy gambler, he was
questioned about drug dealing, and he became a nightly drunk. He
then met a British woman, Doreen Hewitt from Wigan in northern
England, who knew nothing about cycling and had no idea who he
was. She turned his life around and van Steenbergen died, a contented,
grandfatherly figure, in May 2003.

There are for all of us mythical moments which mark us in body and mind, which make others jealous. The queen of classics, Paris–Roubaix, is one of those times. This event, and above all the athletes so rightly called the Giants of the Road, lacks only those other giants, the men beyond measure we know as the Giants of the North. And that's why all the towns of the Nord crossed by Paris–Roubaix have decided to pay homage to the champions of the road. So, along the road this celebrated Sunday in April, through the window, beside the cobbles or on television, we'll see 78 giants made of cloth and wicker saluting the 200 giants made of muscle, sweat and determination.

—Alain Bocquet, regional politician, on introducing
traditional giant dolls in 48 towns in 2004

10
Of Zonzon, Jacques and Rik

France's star in the 1950s was a strong but strange man called Louison Bobet. Even his name was puzzling because to most of France, Louison was a diminutive of Louise and therefore a girl's name. Louison was a boy's name in Brittany, though, and it's what his family called him when he grew up in a baker's shop in St-Méen-le-Grand. In time that, too, is how the rest of the world knew him.

Bobet was respected by other riders but never liked. His habit of weeping in disappointment in his first professional years led him to be called La Bobette behind his back. Bobet had airs of living in a tuxedo, the polished gentleman. It brought him a lot of ribbing from his alter-ego, the rough Raphaël Géminiani, reputed to have tipped a plate of spaghetti on Bobet's head during a restaurant disagreement. Géminiani, adopting the French habit of doubling a syllable of a name to make it affectionate, called him Zonzon. He knew Bobet hated it.

Géminiani mocked Bobet's affectation and love of polite company and its conventions. Bobet even sometimes referred to himself in the third person. He turned down the yellow jersey in the Tour de France in 1947 because it wasn't made of pure wool.

Bobet and Géminiani were obliged to go to a reception and Géminiani smirked as Bobet guarded his manners as he spoke to a society lady.

"Ours is a difficult métier," Géminiani remembered his saying with embarrassment. "You understand, *madame*, that we ride many kilometers a year. It gives us certain difficulties."

Bobet suffered with saddle boils throughout his career. The woman seemed the only person in France not to know.

"Difficulties?" she asked.

"With our…with our…" Bobet blushed. "With our, er, pockets."

"With your pockets, Monsieur Bobet?"

At which point Géminiani exploded and shouted: "Oh, for heaven's sake, Zonzon, tell her you've got bloody balls."

Bobet came to the start of Paris–Roubaix in 1955 as world champion and the previous year's winner of the Tour de France. Beyond doubt that entitled him to respect. He wasn't going to get it from Coppi, who had done all and more than Bobet, but he was used to imposing his will on others. A British rider, Brian Robinson, says Bobet rode up beside him in an everyday village race after the Tour de France—in those days riders like Robinson depended on these races for their living—and told him that he was to let him win or he wouldn't get a contract for the rest of the season.

Bobet therefore didn't appreciate being beaten by Jean Forestier, a former friend with whom he had fallen out. And he erupted against Coppi, whom he said was keener on seeing Bobet lose than on winning himself.

Louison Bobet: a difficult man, but talented

It wasn't a day for being in a good mood. It was cold and wet. Most riders didn't know the route because it had been changed, the towns of Courrières, Carvin, Seclin and Wattignies being dropped in favor of

Courcelles, Évin, Leforest, Mérignies, Pont-à-Marcq and Péronne. The hills around Moncheaux and Mons-en-Pévèle now provided the interest. Only at Ascq did the race come back to its original course.

It was at Mons-en-Pévèle that Forestier attacked. Bobet, Coppi, Hugo Koblet, Jo Planckaert and the few others in the leading group weren't worried. Forestier was talented but, in their estimation, just a good regional rider from Lyons. It was in his hometown that he won a stage of the Tour de France, in 1954.

Forestier, now the oldest living winner of Paris–Roubaix after the death of Émile Masson, said: "I can't say that I was always good, but when I was, I never looked back to see what was happening behind me. I'd felt good that week. When I went training with friends, I was flying. I was the right sort of shape to get over the cobbles. I'm not that tall—1 meter 72—but when I was in shape I weighed 70 kilograms, which was a good combination to get over the cobbles."

Forestier rode on, the name of a little bike factory—Follis—on his jersey, a pump clipped beneath his top tube. And far from losing strength, he jumped between cobbles and sidewalks with grace and held his lead. Bobet grew alarmed and chased. Coppi went with him and also a Frenchman, Gilbert Scodeller.

Scodeller couldn't believe his luck. This was a man who rode three Tours and finished none. He'd won Paris-Tours the previous year but here he was outclassed. But that didn't mean he couldn't win. If Bobet and Coppi could catch Forestier, they'd watch each other and there was a chance he could slip away. If not, he could wait for the finish: he was a good sprinter.

But they never caught Forestier. Coppi wasn't going to help Bobet and then be beaten in a sprint on the track. Bobet wouldn't catch Coppi if he allowed him any distance. But if he *didn't* attack, he'd be prey to Scodeller—to whom he had come second in Paris-Tours.

So the three just rode in together, no one daring to give the other an opening. Forestier won by 15 seconds, Coppi got out of the saddle to sprint, Bobet gave up in disgust and Scodeller came fourth.

Bobet was no longer the genteel man who worried about his "pockets".

"This traitor! This coward!" he protested. "If Coppi had been prepared to work then we'd certainly have caught Forestier because Scodeller was still quite strong. But Coppi was playing to lose and wanted to be sure of being second. In his place, I wouldn't have dared sprint. I was riding to win but Coppi was riding with the sole intention of beating me."

And what happened to Forestier? He won the Ronde van Vlaanderen the following year and, in all, four stages of the Tour de France. In 1957 he became the first Frenchman to wear the green jersey as points leader.

"They were good times," he remembered, "but you had to earn your steak! Nobody got paid a lot and I didn't earn much more than the minimum wage. I survived on the classics and on the village races that followed the Tour."

That was what made Bobet's threat to Robinson, and presumably other lesser riders, so petty.

Jacques Anquetil, to whose team Forestier transferred when Follis stopped sponsoring, went to the start in 1958 with the intention of winning. He was never a man for single-day races. He was a calculator. He had a strange relationship with time, calculating almost to the second how long it would take to ride the time-trials that won him so many stage races, and the time that others would take.

His wife, Janine, said that 2:01 pm to him wasn't the same as 2 pm. He wasn't being difficult: it just wasn't the same time. Raymond Poulidor remembered driving with him on a road where a series of traffic lights were timed to turn green at set intervals, to keep traffic moving but discourage speeding. By the second light Anquetil had calculated the time interval, the distance between the lights and the speed he'd drive to get to each light as it turned green.

"It was a game to him," he said.

Anquetil had won the Tour de France the previous year at his first attempt. He took the lead on the fourth day and, apart from a gap of three days when he lost the yellow jersey to Jean Forestier and then to Nicolas Barone, he led until the end. He won by just four seconds short of a quarter of an hour. He was just 23.

Anquetil was languid. He never put more effort into a race than it demanded. And yet he was never recognized for what he did put into it. Throughout his career his detractors saw him as a dull machine, a robot. Where was the flair of Bobet, the crease-faced suffering of Raymond Poulidor?

It must hurt to win the Tour de France by a margin you could time by a church clock and then be scolded for making it dull. So Anquetil thought he'd ride Paris–Roubaix and stop the tongues turning.

The papers didn't give him much chance. To them, the only certain winner was a stocky Belgian with a melon-slice smile, Rik van Looy. He was already deposing the other Rik, van Steenbergen.

Anquetil got in a break of 20 at St-Just-en-Chaussée. There were 16 away, including Anquetil and Bobet, at Arras. And then with 25 kilometers to go, Anquetil went off alone. There wasn't a rider in the race who could ride alone as fast as Anquetil. He had won the unofficial world time-trial championship, the Grand Prix de Nations, at 19 and he won it again every time he rode. The question of whether he could also master the cobbles was answered when he jumped on and off the sidewalk like a cat.

And then his back tire punctured. The break caught him at Hem.

The race ended in a sprint by 23 riders, something never seen, and went to not van Looy but a lesser Belgian, Léon van Daele. Anquetil was 14th, in the same group, not at all happy. But van Daele was to be less happy still. In winning Paris–Roubaix, he had beaten the favorite— Rik van Looy—who happened to be his captain in the Faema team. Tactics in van Looy's teams were simple: van Looy had to win.

The outcome for van Daele was that his contract with Faema was over and he needed a new team. A chance meeting in a café with Aimé Claeys, who owned the Flandria bike company, led to a team being formed around him for 1959. It was known as Dr Mann-Flandria, the main sponsor being a medical company. It was the birth of a legendary if haphazard team which over the years included Freddy Maertens, Jan Janssen, Joop Zoetemelk, Roger De Vlaeminck, Sean Kelly and even van Looy.

Van Daele repaid the favor by winning Gent-Wevelgem and the team won 44 races that year. Flandria's lasting contribution is that the Japanese component maker, Shimano, created for it its Dura-Ace range. The idea of Japanese bike parts in a world dominated by Campagnolo of Italy seemed laughable.

As for Anquetil, he rode again the following year to take revenge on Roger Rivière, a rider as stylish as he was but both the world pursuit champion and the holder of the world hour record. The two men never got on. Rivère had taunted Anquetil about his poor fitness at the start of the year. There was to be a shoot-out at Paris–Roubaix.

L'Équipe didn't hesitate. Its front page headline was "Van Looy or Rivère." Anquetil made only smaller type lower down. In the end, it was none of them. Anquetil fell at Hénin-Liétard and missed the winning break. Rivère, who'd never before ridden the race, blew up spectacularly faced with the repeated attacks of Fred De Bruyne and Rik van Looy. He trailed in 48th at seven and a half minutes.

Anquetil, who always said that if he were to win a classic it would be Paris–Roubaix, arrived 3 minutes 19 seconds behind the winner, Noël Foré. And who was he? Not one of the biggest names, admittedly, but at the start of a career that included the Tour of Belgium in 1962 and the Ronde van Vlaanderen in 1963.

Anquetil rarely rode classics again. His final disillusion came in Liège–Bastogne–Liège in 1966. He rode it only because he was engaged for two criteriums in Belgium that same week. Raymond Louviot, who shared the management of Anquetil's Ford team with Géminiani, put to him the idea of riding Liège–Bastogne–Liège while he was there.

"It's an idea," Anquetil confessed. "I hadn't thought of it." He hesitated. And then he said: "Will Poulidor be in Belgium?", referring to his greatest French rival. Louviot said he would be. "In that case I'll do it," Anquetil said.

Cycling had introduced dope tests by then, Belgium being the first country in Europe to make drug-taking in sport a crime. Nobody knows if Anquetil took more drugs than anyone else but, unlike others, he made no secret of it. He saw it as a professional right.

Officials demanded a test when he won. He pointed at the showers and said: "Too late. If you can collect it from the soapy water there, go ahead. I'm a human being, not a fountain." The Belgian federation disqualified him, then reinstated him when the case looked like going to law.

Van Looy was also unhappy. By 1961 he had ridden Paris–Roubaix six times without winning. The world championship, yes, the Tour of Lombardy, the Ronde van Vlaanderen, Milan–San Remo, all those… but never Paris–Roubaix. It had become a question of pride.

He presented himself in Paris in his rainbow jersey of world champion. He had won it at Karl-Marx-Stadt, now known as Chemnitz, by the no mean achievement of out-sprinting the Frenchman, André Darrigade.

In Paris–Roubaix, the decision started on the way out of Mons-en-Pévèle. Six riders entered the track together, five Belgians and a Dutchman. Henry Anglade, the little Frenchman who had started the break, was the only absentee: he had punctured at Baisieux. Van Looy won the sprint by jumping out of the final banking. It emerged afterward that his back tire had been going down and he'd been scared of sprinting on the sloped part of the track for fear that it would roll off.

Having done it once, he did it again the next year as well; he also won the world championship again. He rode into Roubaix 25 seconds ahead of the rest, simply riding too fast for the others. And there his happiness ended. For instead of winning a third successive world championship, as seemed likely, van Looy lost after a touch—or was it a tug?—by his team-mate, Benoni Beheyt.

The championship sprint finish at Renaix was a rough-and-tumble affair of swerves, switches and pushes and tugs. The British rider, Tom Simpson, remembered: "I wouldn't have won as there were a number of better sprinters around me but then, bang! Van Looy grabbed me by the jersey and just about brought me to a standstill.

"I managed to get going again, now in the middle of the bunch when, hell's bells! Dutchman Jan Janssen gave me a whacking great pull and just about stopped me completely. I should have gone up and given him a good thump round the ear-hole but what was the use?"

Van Looy was on an off-day and blundered when he started the sprint too soon. Seeing the field moving up on him, he moved across the road, beside Beheyt, but still lost speed. One version was that he was holding off not the opposition but Beheyt, who was riding even faster. Either way, Beheyt put out his right hand and, according to whom you believe, fended off van Looy's saddle or jersey or tugged it so that van Looy lost half a wheel and Beheyt became world champion.

"I'd have ended up in the barriers otherwise," he said.

The row went on all winter. Cynics smiled when van Looy said: "I would have done just the same." He was due to ride at Lokeren the next day but he didn't turn up. He was at home in Herentals, answering neither the phone nor the door to anyone.

He and Beheyt cleaned up in village races for the rest of the year. But after that Beheyt's career was over. Van Looy did all he could to hinder his career, so that he retired at just 26.

The rumpus over Renaix disturbed Belgian cycling the rest of the season and the start of the next. Such was Belgium's fall that journalists predicted a "foreign" win in Paris–Roubaix for the first time in seven years. And they got one.

Van Looy said Paris–Roubaix was his dream for the season—and another chance to deny Beheyt—but other people had the same idea. There were more Italians than usual—Gianni Motta, Ercole Baldini, Italo Ziloli, for instance—and Raymond Poulidor was there for France, and Jan Janssen, although riding for a French team, for Holland. And another Dutchman, Peter Post.

Thirty riders broke clear near Arras, among them Simpson, Zilioli, Janssen and Stablinski. Van Looy and Poulidor were in the next group, at 1 minute 45 seconds. Out of that group came a smaller one, including Beheyt and Post. Together they got up to the leaders. Willy Bocklandt was the first to ride on to the track at Roubaix, Beheyt went past him and then Post went past Beheyt. At 45.131 kilometers per hour for 265 kilometers it was the fastest Paris–Roubaix ever, helped by a tail wind and a declining number of cobbles. It was a meritorious performance but the time had come to go back to how things were. What Paris–Roubaix needed was more cobbles.

There's some scary shit in there. But it's all part of the history and tradition of the race, whether you come in first or 40 minutes behind, like my first time. You get into the velodrome and go into the showers, and De Vlaeminck, Merckx, Hinault—all these legends have been in there before you, and you're scrubbing mud out of your ears. It's all part of the adventure.

—Stuart O'Grady

11

The Order Changes

In 1966, Paris–Roubaix became Chantilly–Roubaix, at least on the map. It moved out of Paris and off to the east to include cobbles that mayors hadn't seen the need to resurface. And in 1968 it took in Jean Stablinski's road through the Arenberg forest.

The Arenberg created a sensation. The British journalist, Jock Wadley, arrived in France to find newspapers predicting "only 30 at most will finish this race. Even fewer if it rains." Another suggested riders would need a sprung saddle, padded bars and fat wired-on tires to finish in the first 10. One official said nobody would finish at all if it rained.

There were now 57 kilometers of cobbles. The 15 kilometers between Templeuve and Bachy had almost no tar at all.

Pascal Sergent wrote: "The press announced that the 1968 edition would be, without doubt, the most difficult and the most extraordinary in history and that the Queen of Classics would see a legendary winner in the style of cycling's heroic period."

It remained to see who it would be, for the order was changing. Where Rik van Steenbergen had had to succumb to Rik van Looy, now van Looy was also threatened. Eddy Merckx had won "his" world championship. Van Looy's not inconsiderable pride was dented.

In 1965 Merckx had been in van Looy's Solo-Superia team, sponsored by a margarine company and a bike maker. But he had committed the crime of threatening his boss and he moved to the French team, Peugeot. There he won Milan–San Remo for the first of seven times. But Peugeot was skinflint and its riders had to buy their own wheels and tires. It wasn't hard to move to a new team supported by Faema, an Italian maker of coffee machines returning to the sport. And there, 1967, he became world champion.

Van Looy was grudging. When Merckx started 1968 badly, losing Milan–San Remo and abandoning Paris–Nice, he scoffed: "If Merckx is the boss, let him prove it." The two were so wary of each other in the break in the GP E3 in Belgium that Jacques de Boever won instead. De Boever had never won a decent race in his life and never did again.

Before Paris–Roubaix, van Looy, now 35, said he was delighted by the tougher route. "It will make the legs of the young hurt," he said pointedly.

Nerves in the peloton made the first break go at 17 kilometers. It had four minutes by Solesmes. There, riders seemed almost surprised to find cobbles. They got going just as the break began flagging. News of their weakening came back via the blackboard man and Merckx attacked, taking 13 others with him. The notable exception was van Looy.

At Coutiches, Merckx looked over his shoulder and counted. There were too many. He attacked. Only Ward Sels and Willy Bocklandt stayed with him. Of those, Sels was the greater worry. He was a sprinter of Rik van Looy's level and sometimes his lead-out man. A little later things grew worse with the arrival of the mournful-looking Herman van Springel, whom any film director would cast perfectly as a pallbearer. Van Springel didn't have the same talent but Merckx was now fighting on two fronts.

Imagine, then, his relief when Sels punctured 26 kilometers from the finish. Merckx hunched his shoulders and spread his elbows in a style that was just becoming familiar and attacked. Van Springel had to sprint out of every corner to hold his back wheel. Merckx swooped past his rival at the finish by rising to the top of the banking at the finish and accelerating down and past him. He won, his right arm raised, by a wheel.

It was the beginning of the end for van Looy. Three punctures had done nothing to help his chances but the eclipse was starting. It's not even sure what happened to him. Pascal Sergent says he was in a group sprinting for ninth place, eight minutes down. The result shows the sprint was for eighth, but that matters less than that van Looy's name isn't there at all. He rode just once more, in 1969, came 22nd and never rode it again.

And the Arenberg? An anticlimax. Merckx finished with barely a splash of mud on his white jersey.

There had never been a talent like Eddy Merckx's. He is the only rider to have sent the sport into recession through his own success. Riders became disillusioned because they rarely raced for anything better than second place. Their salaries fell because sponsors saw little value

Eddy Merckx: so good he put the sport into recession

in backing a team they knew would be beaten. And contract fees for village races tumbled because promoters had to pay so much for Merckx, whose simple presence guaranteed a crowd and advertisers, that there was less left for the rest. And this continued for season after season.

For him, Paris–Roubaix was just one classic among many. "I took a particular interest in my equipment," he said, "especially if the forecast was for rain but, for me, it was a classic like the rest, with its own demands and a particular character."

In 1970 he won Paris–Roubaix by more than five minutes. The rain fell, lightning was forecast over the northern plains, and riders fell and tore skin. Jean-Marie Leblanc, who went on to organize the Tour de France, broke his frame. Merckx left the Arenberg forest with six riders behind him. He punctured at Bouvignies, 56 kilometers from the finish, changed a wheel, re-caught the leaders and went straight back to the front. And, before long, off the front. He won by 5 minutes 20 seconds.

In second place that day—and fifth the year before—was a dark-haired, gypsy-looking man with long sideburns: Roger De Vlaeminck.

"In a country in love with Eddy Merckx to the point of servitude," said the writer Olivier Dazat, "literally dead drunk on his repeated exploits, the showers of stones and thorns from the Gypsy constituted, along with the Mannequin Pis [the statue in Brussels of a small boy peeing], the last bastion of independence and humor, a refusal of uniformity in a conquered land."

De Vlaeminck—it's pronounced *Roshay De Vlah-mink*—won 16 classics and 22 stages of major Tours. He rode Paris–Roubaix 10 times and always finished, four times in first place. The only laurels he lacked were a world road championship and, because he was only a moderate climber, a big stage race.

He had a characteristic position. He crouched low across the top tube, his hands on the brake hoods, his elbows lower than his wrists. It provided bounce, springing against the shocks. When he got going seriously, he lowered his hands to the bends of his bars and pushed his body horizontal, a cyclo-cross man turned track pursuiter. He gave, said Olivier Dazat, "the impression of gliding, of being in a perpetual search for speed, like a skier perfecting his schluss."

The weather in 1972 was apocalyptic. It drizzled throughout the race. Water lay between the cobbles and, more treacherously, on the irregular sides of the roads, hiding missing stones, displacing others under the weight of the cars and motorbikes that preceded the riders. There could be no worse setting for the Arenberg. The break entered it at full speed as usual, riders trying to get there first to avoid piling into fallen riders.

Their speed in the rain brought down a heap of riders, including Merckx. De Vlaeminck rode on and feinted an attack where the old mining road rejoins the tar. The others matched him and he sat up. It allowed Merckx to catch them.

There was a brief hope that a local would win when Alain Santy, a northerner, got clear with Willy van Malderghem, winner of the previous year's Quatre Jours de Dunkerque. His moment lasted until 35 kilometers from the end, when his weakness showed. Van Malderghem pushed on alone with more than a minute and half in hand.

De Vlaeminck waited. The lead stayed unchanged. Then he set off and caught van Malderghem at Cysoing, dangerously close to the end. He pressed on and crossed the line, his left hand raised, a fraction less than two minutes ahead of André Dierickx and 2 minutes 13 seconds before Barry Hoban. Merckx was seventh at 2 minutes 39 seconds.

De Vlaeminck said: "When you're really fit, you rarely get a flat tire because you're more lucid. I had a puncture once, in 1970, and then never again in 10 years. The other secret is confidence. I often started with the idea that I was going to win. I missed my chance once or twice but no more than that. I knew how to get ready for Paris–Roubaix. I used to ride three days of 350 kilometers a day in the week before. I used to ride Gent–Wevelgem and then ride another 130 kilometers having just changed my jersey. One year I rode 430 kilometers in a day. I needed that, that sort of training, to start the race in a good frame of mind."

He'd got it right. In 1974 he won by 57 seconds, ahead of Francesco Moser, who had crashed.

De Vlaeminck rode now for Brooklyn, a team sponsored by a chewing gum maker owned by brothers named Perfetti. The team—he rode there with his brother Erik and with Patrick Sercu—wore a garish jersey based on the American flag. The curious thing was that for all the American connections in the name and jersey, and the image of the Brooklyn bridge, the chewing gum sold in the USA only three decades after the team folded.

And why did it fold? Because a member of the Perfetti family was kidnapped and there was no money left for a team after paying the ransom.

By now, De Vlaeminck had started training in secret. His technique was straightforward if arduous: "I used to get up at 5am. When it was good weather I went out behind a Derny with my lights on. I used to meet Godefroot to go training and I'd already ridden 120 kilometers. I used to pretend that I was tired because I'd just got out of bed and try to persuade him we should have a shorter ride together. I don't know if I took him in but I needed to bluff the others to raise my own morale."

Godefroot trained with De Vlaeminck because the schisms in Belgium cycling meant he never spoke to Merckx. He said of De Vlaeminck: "In the evening he'd call me to ask me if we could go out later than we'd agreed. 'It's not worth doing too much,' he used to say to me. The next day, he'd get up at six, train for two hours behind a Derny, and then he'd turn up at the rendezvous as though nothing had happened. That was Roger."

In 1975, April 13 started dull with an occasional beam of sun. It had rained the previous days, though, and the race hit a bog of wet mud when it reached the first cobbles at Neuvilly. Chaos followed. Cars got stuck in the swamp at the side of the road and motorcyclists came sliding off. Riders who stayed upright picked their way through and the field shattered. By the time the cobbles ended there were just six in the lead. De Vlaeminck wasn't there but he came up a little later with Merckx, and then at the approach to Valenciennes, they were joined by a group including Francesco Moser.

There were four by Roubaix, all Belgian. Merckx began the sprint on the back straight. De Vlaeminck looked beaten but struggled back. He passed Merckx just before the line and won with his pedals opposite Merckx's front tire. He didn't even have time to lift his arm.

"It's nice to win," he said, "especially when Merckx is beaten."

André Dierickx was third and Marc Demeyer came fourth.

It was the following year that Demeyer both won and started promoting another brand of chewing gum, Stimorol, from Denmark. The success that caused such an exciting advertisement on Radio Mi Amigo wasn't a surprise; in 1975 he had ridden alone in the lead for 50 kilometers. He was a gentle giant, Demeyer. He turned professional in

1972 with almost casual disregard, spreading his contract on the roof of a car just before a race. And, equally casually he then won the race, the Dwars door België.

Demeyer spent most of his short life as lead-out man for Freddy Maertens. He could win races for himself, as Paris–Roubaix proved in 1976, but he was self-effacing by nature and happy to ride as Maertens' *knecht*, closing gaps and opening sprints.

There was no greater bitterness than between Maertens and his fans and the Eddy Merckx camp. They were opposites, Maertens the near-unbeatable sprinter and Merckx the *rouleur*.

Philippe Brunel of *L'Équipe* asked Merckx if it was true what journalists wrote, that there was an anti-Merckx brigade.

"And how!" he answered. "You've only got to remember the names of the riders there were at Flandria: Godefroot, the De Vlaeminck brothers, Dierickx, Leman, and then later on, Maertens. They all rode against me."

De Vlaeminck's response was: "It's simple: we were *all* against him. Even my wife! During meals with the Flandria team, Merckx was all we spoke about, from morning to evening, to work out what we were going to do to beat him."

That was the atmosphere when Paris–Roubaix set off for the 74th time, delayed by a protest which blocked the start. It got away only after the demonstrators had deflated all the tires on the car which Félix Lévitan, the co-organizer, had been expecting to drive. He considered the situation with a mixture of anger and puzzled offense. What had *he* done to upset the demonstrators, beyond giving them a piece of his mind?

The Belgian civil war between Merckx and Maertens reached an armistice when both fell off at Neuvilly. Maertens abandoned the race and Merckx finished sixth at 1 minute 36 seconds. Freed from his duty to Maertens, Demeyer had a free hand.

De Vlaeminck wanted the race, of course, and tried to split it by sending away two teammates. Johann Demuynck and Marcello Osler stayed away through the Arenberg cobbles but impressed few into chasing. Guy Sibille rode alone in the lead for 35 kilometers but that threatened nobody. Who on earth was this Sibille man, anyway? He'd come third in Milan–San Remo the previous year but he'd never won better than stages in regional tours. He did, in fact, win the 1976 French national championship, but that came after rather than before Paris–Roubaix. The others could ignore him, and they did—for three-quarters of an hour.

In the end, De Vlaeminck sorted things out for himself. There were still 30 kilometers to go. He went so decisively that Merckx couldn't go with him, his legs and will hurt by having to change bikes five times and chase back to the leaders each time. Francesco Moser was there, though, and so were Godefroot and the lightly stammering Hennie Kuiper—and Marc Demeyer.

But De Vlaeminck was overconfident. He mastered Moser's efforts to dislodge him and no longer had to worry about Godefroot, who had flatted a tire. He led on to the track, sure he had the best sprint. But he'd ridden too hard in the last 30 minutes and he'd gambled too much on the final dash for the line. Moser came past him and then Demeyer came by them both.

"They just sat on my wheel for the last 20 kilometers," De Vlaeminck said miserably.

On January 20, 1982, Marc Demeyer went training for 100 kilometers in the morning, then went to collect new equipment from his team manager, Bert De Kimpe, boss of a team supported by Splendor, a bike company whose sponsorship went back to 1936.

That evening he was sitting at home, doing a crossword. He never finished it. He had a heart attack and died. He was 31. He is buried in the Outrijve churchyard at Alveringem, 40 kilometers east of Ypres in West Flanders.

The first rule is to ride the cobbles on the drops of the bars. That lets you stay stable on the bike. But it's hard to keep in that position. Your back aches so much because you're more used to riding on the top of the bars or on the brake hoods. So to get used to it, I ride long sessions on the bottom of the bars, but it's hard.

—Jimmy Engoulvent, 2004

12

But for the Money, It Could Have Been Five

Freddy Maertens smiles. The one race he never won was the one he most wanted: the Ronde van Vlaanderen. The irony is that he works at the Ronde's museum in the main square at Oudenaarde.

Maertens towed Roger De Vlaeminck round the race in 1977. They reached the Koppenberg, akin to the worst cobbles of Paris–Roubaix but on a steep rise as well, and there Maertens' brother gave him a change of bike. The rules didn't allow it but officials couldn't get alongside him to tell him until the Paterstraat, some distance on.

Maertens version is that "A man at the Belgian federation and the UCI had something against me, so he disqualified me. He said 'You are out of the race.' That would normally mean you had to stop, but he didn't say 'Stop!' I asked Lomme Driessens [the Flandria manager] and he said to go on because it would be good publicity."

Maertens rode on and towed a doubting De Vlaeminck to victory, sitting up at the end because he knew he'd been disqualified. They were two minutes ahead of the rest. De Vlaeminck had no idea whether, having ridden with a rider who wasn't supposed to be there, he too would be thrown out.

Maertens smiles because "when visitors come to the museum, they always remember the 1977 race. If you ask them who won another year, they have to think about it. But, '77, everyone says 'It was you and De Vlaeminck.'"

On the windowsill on the edge of the museum, so that they face into the street, are a row of cobbles. Each carries the name of a year's winner. For 1977 there are two. The lower one names De Vlaeminck. The one above it reads: "Moral winner, Freddy Maertens." The moral winner is still angry that De Vlaeminck didn't pay the money that Maertens says, but De Vlaeminck denies, they decided for the two to the finish.

Freddy Maertens with his "moral winner" cobble

Maertens wanted revenge in Paris–Roubaix. De Vlaeminck was a good rider, he acknowledged: "He won a lot of races—but he was never world champion too." Maertens was world champion in 1976 and 1981.

De Vlaeminck, equally, needed to show that he owed his Ronde van Vlaanderen to nobody. And that was the atmosphere in which Paris–Roubaix started in 1977. The year in which Maertens rode as world champion. The year in which everyone fell off. Or so it seemed. And the year, incidentally, when the start moved from Chantilly to Compiègne because yet more roads had been surfaced and Albert Bouvet needed more room to take the race along fresh cobbles.

Gérard Moneyron brought down the first great heap of riders when he slipped on the first cobbles, at Neuvilly. He took down Moser and a fast improving Dutchman, Jan Raas. More falls followed. Moser went down again. Down, too, went Bernard Thévenet—and Maertens, who punctured twice and fell off once.

There were 22 in the leading group with 35 kilometers to ride. The atmosphere was tense. Demeyer attacked to open the way for Maertens, but it came to nothing. Then De Vlaeminck tried, taking Moser before getting clear alone. Maertens was third on the road with 1,000 meters to go but he was already more than a minute and a half behind.

De Vlaeminck said he thought more of his third place behind Demeyer than he did of his fourth win. That was fine and dandy, to be sure, but he was followed by what Jacques Goddet branded in *L'Équipe* as a bunch of defeatists. His victory should have been worth more than that, Goddet wrote.

So, could he have won a fifth time? Perhaps he could.

It may have been that afternoon in the showers beside the track that De Vlaeminck talked to Moser—who came 13th just behind an aging Raymond Poulidor—about his future. The money had run out in the Brooklyn team and De Vlaeminck was looking to go elsewhere. Until now he had ridden only for Belgian teams. They were notoriously haphazard. Italians looked so much more polished, well managed, well equipped and better advised. So for 1978 De Vlaeminck rode for Sanson, an ice cream maker.

The team had 16 riders, all Italian except for three Belgians and an Englishman, Phil Edwards. For De Vlaeminck, the decision was simple. He went for the money. He said: "It turned out a bad decision because we didn't have the same objectives. Moser is a natural, a great champion, but he has an ego. We never used to speak. Moser had eight teammates and me. I had to sort myself out, which cost me Paris–Roubaix in 1978. Moser attacked where I'd planned to attack, on the cobbles at Bachy, 20 kilometers from Roubaix. I had to respect the team's loyalties so I turned round to Raas and offered him a lot of money if he'd chase instead. He did. He tried all he could but when Moser went away, there wasn't much you could do about it."

The outcome was that De Vlaeminck came second by 1 minute 40 seconds with the obliging Raas just behind him.

The same thing happened the following year as well, Moser first again and De Vlaeminck second this time by 40 seconds. The Belgian's star was fading. That famous lucidity was going and, with it, the saintly protection from falls and flats. In 1980 he punctured 24 kilometers before the finish and then fell off. For the first time in 12 races, he abandoned.

For decades Belgians had had the run of not just Paris–Roubaix but of many one-day races. France had been hindered by a rule compelling riders to stay amateur until they had finished their stint in the army. The intention was to improve France's chances in the Olympics and world championships but the result was to weaken an already aging professional peloton. But that didn't explain why Belgium should be so much better.

Pierre Chany pointed out that Belgium had only a fifth the population of France. In fact the contrast was still greater because most of Belgium's top riders came from only the northern, Dutch-speaking half of the country.

"In this area of Flanders," he wrote, "where austerity is the general rule, cycling is part of daily life. Bike races are to the Flemish as bull-fighting is to Andalucia, baseball to Yankees, ice hockey to Canadians, pétanque to Provence. In Latin countries, cycling is a sport, a distraction, whereas around Waregem and Kortrijk it's a religion—a religion which holds its services in village streets, several times a week, and a Flemish family without a cyclist is just a little ashamed."

A French schoolboy who turns to athletics or football is encouraged and praised, he said. But pick cycling instead and he gets a poor mark even in physical education. In Belgium, by contrast, he'd be encouraged and congratulated if he got good results.

"This is a micro-country with a dense population, which means daily contact between riders, coaches and organizers. A young rider never has to train alone. He has only to knock on a neighbor's door to find a riding partner. On the road he'll meet riders like Godefroot, Dierickx,

Verbeeck, Leman or De Vlaeminck, and he can jump in behind them and they won't refuse to give him advice…

"A Belgian amateur is already a professional; a French professional stays an amateur for a long time."

And yet the circle turns. Did anyone realize how much changed in 1981? It wasn't just the end of the De Vlaeminck era or even of Moser's. There was more, although how much more wasn't clear until later.

Bernard Hinault was world champion. He looked happy enough as he stood on the podium in his rainbow jersey but he was a bitter man.

"Paris–Roubaix is a *connerie!*" he snapped. Hinault was never a man to mess with words. *Connerie* isn't easy to translate but it's a heavy insult, something more than simply stupid. And to emphasize his feelings, he told journalists: "There's no point in insisting, you won't get me to take my words back—Paris–Roubaix is a *connerie.*"

He hadn't even started in a good mood. "The people who want me to win at any cost aren't the people who are going to have to ride it," he said. Philippe Brunel of *L'Équipe* suspected the only reason he rode at all was to match Merckx, "to satisfy history and not to be in debt to Eddy Merckx, whom he was finding it difficult to follow." It's a view shared by Pierre Chany. "An inner voice kept telling him he had to try or stay a marginal champion compared to Coppi and Merckx," he said.

It had been 25 years since a Frenchman had won. If Hinault didn't want to match Merckx in his year as world champion then he wanted to go down in history as the equal of Louison Bobet, winner quarter of a century earlier. Now he was cross that other people thought the same thing. "I don't go into offices and tell people to work harder," he said, "yet people ask me to be the strongest on the cobbles."

He says now that it wasn't hatred. More, it was his memory of Paris–Roubaix in 1979, when he was dropped because of a puncture, and above all of that year's Tour de France. Jacques Goddet had wanted a Tour with everything, and that included the cobbles of the north. Hinault punctured and had to chase in vain for 109 kilometers. He lost three and a half minutes and the yellow jersey to Joop Zoetemelk.

At Paris–Roubaix he told journalists he took races as they came, that Paris–Roubaix was a bit harder than the rest but that it was just a race like the rest.

"I've never made Paris–Roubaix one of my season's objectives," he said. "It's the press that's done that." Which makes you wonder where the press got the idea. As Noël Coudel, head of cycling at *L'Équipe* put it, Hinault had won just about everything else and Paris–Roubaix was the one missing jewel in his crown. How could anybody believe that it wasn't an objective?

Hinault and his team traveled to Noyon three days before Paris–Roubaix. They went training in sunshine, Hinault already on edge. Pascal Poisson, a domestique, rode behind him, whistling to annoy him. A scooter went by. Hinault told him he wasn't going to be whistling much longer and set off to chase it. "Soon everyone was in a line behind me; nobody was whistling any more."

The team went to Compiègne in the team bus, watching a blue movie. They were nervous; they had trained in good weather but overnight it had poured and the roads had turned to swamps.

Hinault fell seven times that day, April 12. Attack after attack pushed the speed for the first hour to 45.2 kilometers per hour. Fifteen kilometers from the finish a black dog with a red collar broke free of its owner and went snapping at the riders. Hinault was leading the group, De Vlaeminck behind him, then Moser, Hennie Kuiper and Dirk De Meyer. The others had a glimpse of what was happening but Hinault hit the dog with his front wheel and crashed to the ground. He got up, swearing and hurting, tried his bike and set off after the others.

A wonderful picture shows him in his rainbow jersey at the Tranchée d'Arenberg, not riding but running through a field behind the crowd with his bike on his shoulder, number 40 pinned to each hip. Félix Lévitan's red car had been held up by a crash and it blocked the road.

"I took a short-cut through the garden," Hinault explained, meaning the field behind the crowd. A photographer noticed but barely anybody else. His photo shows the crowd staring at the road, at the heap of riders, while the world champion runs behind them. A young boy with fair hair and his back to the camera has spotted him because he was two paces back from the crowd. Hinault ran in front of him. Apart from him, the only others of the crowd of two dozen to see him are a tall man with a Beatle haircut, a slim blonde with a cardigan hooked over her shoulders and a curly-haired, crumple-faced grandmother in a flowery dress and thick stockings. It's impossible to know whether she's surprised, cross or just put out that she's going to have to get out of Hinault's way.

Hinault won the sprint at Roubaix, winding up a 53 x 13 gear for a whole lap and leaving no scope for the rest. The effort proved exhausting and he wavered off a straight line in the last meters. Marc Demeyer tried to squeeze through the gap that he left but without succeeding.

The Frenchman was still seething: "I'm not taking a word back of what I said!"

De Vlaeminck should have won it, being the better sprinter. But... "I paid for the sin of over-confidence," he said. "When I rode on to the track, I was sure I was going to win and so I lost. Hinault went off in the front and I couldn't get up to him because Roubaix isn't a real track but a cement circuit were you can wind up a big gear."

He said of Hinault that he, Raas and a few others could win Paris–Roubaix because they were great riders "but they weren't especially talented on the cobbles. It's a question of style. They were too stiff on their bikes, not supple enough. This may shock you but even Eddy Merckx wasn't a man for the cobbles. He won three times because he's Merckx and he had that depth of talent. That's what counts in the end, otherwise a cyclo-cross specialist like Roland Liboton would have won. My brother, Erik, didn't have that depth, that resistance."

Erik De Vlaeminck, as fair as Roger was dark and with a round, slightly absent-minded face, was the best cyclo-cross rider the world has seen. He won the world championship seven times between 1966 and 1973. The year he missed—1967—was because his bike broke. In 1968 Erik was the professional and Roger the amateur champion.

The explanation of why cyclo-cross riders don't do better in a classic which ought to suit them goes unanswered. Cyclo-cross favors light riders and Paris–Roubaix favors greater weight and strength to keep the bike from bouncing on the cobbles or bogging down in the mud. But neither of the De Vlaeminck brothers was either short or skeletal.

To get back to Hinault, though, there was a nice touch at the end. He said: "I'm not a great one for anniversaries, but this was one that I intended to celebrate. I became the first French winner of Paris–Roubaix for 25 years. Louison Bobet was present in Roubaix when I won, as if he'd had a premonition of what might happen a quarter of a century later."

Hinault rode again next year, to show his face and honor the previous year's victory. He came ninth and had the dismay of seeing the victory go to Jan Raas, a rider he couldn't stand. After all his complaints about the race, there is a gentle irony in that Hinault now works for the organizers and presents the cobble to each year's winner. But there is, accord-

Bernard Hinault: talented but too stiff on his bike, said De Vlaeminck

ing to many, damage as well. The generation that started cycling when Hinault called the race a *connerie* is the generation that now stays away. It is as if France's last hero, a world champion, five times winner of the Tour de France, gave them license to watch the race on TV instead.

Philippe Brunel wrote in *L'Équipe*: "We won't go as far as to say that the five-time winner of the Tour—who every year gives the winner his celebration cobble stone on behalf of the organizers—has contributed to the dilution [*paupérisation*] of the queen of classics, which would offend him, but his words have contributed to the snub, or the indifference, of those who stay away.

"The fact isn't new but the phenomenon is getting worse and is concerning. The peloton of stay-aways has grown to the point where Paris–Roubaix is now only for a tight group of specialists...especially the Belgians, capable of maintaining high speed on the cobbles. In 2002 only two of the top 20 riders in the UCI table—Jens Voigt and Erik Zabel—were on the line. The following year only Zabel was there. In 2004 he had stayed at home as well."

The creation of a world points competition in 1989 split the sport. There were those who concentrated on stage races and those who chased the classics. Some rarely saw each other all year. Miguel Indurain and Lance Armstrong, who won 12 Tours de France between them, not only ignored Paris–Roubaix but any other race they felt inconvenient. Paulo Bettini, who won the World Cup three times, never rode Paris–Roubaix.

Eddy Merckx added: "It's a shame to say it, but Paris–Roubaix is losing more and more of its value because the great riders aren't there. I've always said that to win without risk is to win without glory. In my era, even Poulidor rode Paris–Roubaix. Even Ocaña. The stars didn't worry about risking their prestige on the cobbles. Now, Ullrich, Armstrong, Vinokourov think only of the Tour. But the Tour isn't the whole of cycling. And anyway I don't think Paris–Roubaix is any more dangerous than other races. Apart from Museeuw and Gaumont, accidents are rare. Paris–Roubaix will go on for as long as there are cobbles, but it's in danger. And you have to ask yourself if it's worth preserving the cobbles if they only interest a handful of riders, if those who stay away think it's old-fashioned and out of date? That's the problem."

The accidents to Johan Museeuw and Philippe Gaumont happened on the Tranchée d'Arenberg. It is the road that has done much to add interest to the race but also much to keep riders away.

In 1998, Johan Museeuw broke his kneecap and in 2001 Philippe Gaumont broke his thigh.

Museeuw fell and collapsed sideways, his knee pointing outwards. It hit the sharp edge of a cobble and the kneecap split in two. That was serious enough but things grew worse when infection set in. Surgeons considered amputating the leg. Some reports say he came close to losing his life. It certainly took him 10 months to recover. And then a car accident in 2000 put him in a coma for 20 days. He was 200 meters from his home in Gistel, riding a motorbike with his wife and daughter. He and a car collided at a junction. Museeuw broke his skull, collarbone and a knee.

In Gaumont's case, he had decided to "make the selection", as French puts it, and he was riding flat out. The driver of his team car, Alain Deloeuil, shouted at him to calm down. Gaumont's team-mates, Nico Mattan and Chris Peers, got to his side and shouted "We're finished!"

Gaumont shouted back that he was on "a day of grace", that he was flying like never before.

"Stop it! That's enough!", Deloeuil shouted at him. And then Gaumont fell. The crack of broken bone was audible even above the noise of the race. Gaumont didn't move. Deloeuil stopped his car by the road, knowing the danger it would cause but realising the danger to his rider was even greater. His mechanic, Érik Rouzé, reached Gaumont as other riders negotiated a way around him.

"He was howling," Rouzé remembered. "Immediately he said 'My leg—it's broken!'"

The ambulance that followed the race arrived once the bulk of the field had passed. It took him to the hospital in Valenciennes. There doctors found his kneecap forced to the right of his leg and a great blister of blood on his leg.

"Breaking your femur is serious for anyone," Gaumont said, "but an open break in an athlete of high level at full effort, that tears the muscles. At 180 heart beats a minute, there's a colossal loss of blood, which meant my leg was completely filled with blood. Luckily the artery wasn't touched."

Doctors operated that night and fitted a 40 centimeter screw that ran up the bone and held it together. It was fastened at the head of the femur with a 12 millimeter screw. He stayed immobile in his bed for a month and a half. He lost 7 kilograms, much of it through atrophy of his muscles.

Museeuw's broken kneecap became infected and he came close to losing his leg. Others have ridden on regardless. Jacques Bossis, for example, in 1981.

"I'd really trained hard for it. I'd just finished third in Milan-San Remo. Well, halfway through the race there were 30 of us at the front.

All the strong guys were there. And then suddenly Kuiper went to the side and there was a crash.

"I fell really heavily on my elbow. The doctor looked after the cut and I set off again. I could feel a sharp pain in my shoulder blade. I'd lost two minutes. I set off chasing the leaders again. I made a big effort and I got back up with the leaders. And then a short time later on a bend, a new crash on my painful side. My shoulder blade really hurt now. A spectator tried to get me upright and I insulted him. And then I realized what I'd said, how unfair I'd been to this kind man and I apologised.

"I got back on my bike and I finished 33rd at Roubaix. I'd just ridden 80 kilometers with a broken shoulder blade. Bernard Hinault won. Without my falls I would have been up with him in the sprint. That day, I wore number 13 in the race. I refused to be number 13 again for ever more."

The reputation of the Arenberg is that nobody has won the race there, but plenty have lost it. The 2005 Paris–Roubaix skipped it for the first time since 1968. For some it had become just too dangerous. The cobbles grew worse still after that and, although the race then went in the opposite direction to avoid the uncontrollable speed of the descent, the organizers decided to drop the road from 2005 until it could be made ridable again.

Nico Mattan said: "Every year recently I have lost around 40 seconds in the *tranchée* [the Arenberg]. When you see a friend fall, when you hear him cry out in pain, when you know how long it will take for him to get back to health, you can no longer ride as hard as you used to or without the Arenberg."

He was referring to Gaumont.

"Paris–Roubaix will stay a mythical race and I dream of winning like a warrior, my helmet on crooked, my face covered in grime and my body covered in wounds. But the wounds of the Arenberg have always been too deep."

On the other hand, Marc Madiot, the winner in 1991, said: "If you make everything antiseptic, if you want to eliminate every risk, then little by little you'll kill the beauty of the sport. So, people say that the Arenberg only makes riders *lose* the race? And so what? That's pretty impressive in itself. And even if the race was just as interesting even if it didn't go through there, it's the principle that annoys me. They've already put barriers on both sides of the road, which has robbed the place of a lot of its identity.

"The Arenberg is a moment of history, the moment that defines the sport, a moment of communion, of madness, of real contact between the people and the riders. Before, when spectators came too close, you could avoid them, slalom on the edges of the road. That was the adventure of it. If you take away all that, you eliminate the unexpected, the spark."

In *Nord-Éclair* he summed it up in a few words: "Paris–Roubaix without the Arenberg would be like the Vendée Globe without the icebergs." The Vendée Globe is a round-the-world yacht race known for its dangers.

The Arenberg cobbles returned in 2006, scoured clean and widened at the entrance. Their absence had been noted. Christian Prudhomme, cycling director at the Amaury Sport Organisation which promotes the race, said that in 2005 "we witnessed a linear race, limpid, without it."

At the start of the seventies we used to go to bars along the course. We used to talk over mugs of beer. We'd get out all our maps. There'd be Albert Bouvet, Jean Stablinski, Édouard Delberghe, Bernard Vandecasteele, Jean Montois, and all the guys who came from the area. The first two had just found the path through Wallers-Arenberg. We we were explorers of times gone by.

—Jean-Claude Vallaeys, president of *Les Amis de Paris–Roubaix*, 2002, on finding fresh cobbles.

13

Feeling Happy,
Feeling Sad

Edwin Noel Plowden isn't a man who often turns up in cycling histories and so it ought to be explained that he was Britain's wartime head of aircraft production. In 1959 he was made Lord Plowden and he became chairman of Tube Investments, a manufacturing group which included the British Cycle Corporation. Such was the state of cycling in Britain that BCC or its rival, Raleigh, took over one ailing company after another and in the end the two of them merged.

Plowden was important enough that he was to be met at airports. The day came when fog diverted him to one airport when TI's other bigwigs had gone to another. Nobody from Raleigh could go so he was met by the staff of Carlton Cycles, a company some miles away which made Raleigh's racing bikes.

Carlton was run by brothers, Kevin and Gerald O'Donovan, sons of an Irish motorbike-maker and racer. They collected Plowden and brought him to their factory. "I think he was a bit taken aback to have his hand shaken by oily palms, to be chatted up by smiling workers and to be asked for his autograph," Gerald O'Donovan recalled. "My lads made the most of having a live Lord to themselves and I wasn't above taking advantage of it myself."

Raleigh was known for supporting track riders, particularly the sprinter, Reg Harris. Other than an incidental involvement with a German team, Ruberg, it knew little of road racing beyond an early meeting with a young amateur called Tom Simpson, whom the company helped. But then in 1964 a Sheffield enthusiast called George

Shaw brought Kevin O'Donovan an idea for a semipro team in Britain. O'Donovan liked the idea but he needed more money. He pulled in a favor. He called Lord Plowden.

It was a successful call. Plowden's enthusiasm, to the extent of lending his jet, extended to putting a full team on the continent. Britain had entered the European Common Market and Raleigh saw its future there. It took on as manager the man who won that fastest Paris–Roubaix of all: Peter Post.

Post ran TI-Raleigh with such discipline that its abbreviation of "TI-R Group" was turned by the peloton into *Tirgroup*, a play on "firing squad." He had become a modern Ludo Feuillet. And under that direction, from 1976 to 1983, Raleigh won two world road championships (Gerrie Knetemann 1978, Raas 1979), the 1980 Tour de France (Zoetemelk), the Amstel Gold Race in 1978, 1979 and 1980, the Tour of Flanders in 1979 and Gent–Wevelgem in 1980. Plus 15 world championships, five World Cups, 77 Tour stages, the Giro d'Italia, 37 classics and 55 national championships.

It also won Paris–Roubaix in 1982, producing a happy winner, whistles at the finish, and an unhappy loser.

The winner was Jan Raas, the Dutchman that Hinault couldn't stand. He and Hinault were in the break 20 kilometers from Roubaix, along

Jan Raas: not popular among riders but undeniably classy

with an aging Roger De Vlaeminck and a handful of other riders including Raas's Belgian team-mate, Ludo Peeters. Post's direction and bonding of the Raleigh team had got the two into the lead in the first place. Now it had to be decided what was to happen next.

The obvious move was that Peeters, the weaker of the two Raleigh riders, would accelerate away alone. And he did. Raas sat and watched Hinault. The Frenchman had a problem. He could catch Peeters but only with Raas tacking on to his wheel. Raas would not only be fresher at Roubaix but he would have Peeters to lead him out in the sprint. But if Hinault *didn't* chase, then Peeters would win, Raas would probably come second and the best that Hinault could hope for was third.

Well, it was victory or it was third. In fact if he did nothing at all, it could even be fourth or fifth. And so he chased, Raas as expected sheltering behind him and doing nothing to help. Hinault caught Peeters on the final hill, at Hem. A Swiss rider, Stefan Mutter, had been in the train behind Hinault and he tried his chance. He got 50 meters. And then Raas sprinted up to and past him.

Indecision gripped the rest and Raas won alone, two hands high above his bespectacled face. The crowd cheered and it whistled. Belgian spectators were unexcited because a Dutchman had won. And they had seen the way Peeters had been used as a chopping block by a Dutchman. There's often little love between Belgians and their northern neighbours. The French had seen the little known Yvon Bertin come second, which was good, but they had also seen Hinault finish a disillusioned ninth, which was bad.

Peeters never got over the disappointment. "It was the day my team caused me to lose the race," he said sadly. "Even if they later helped me win other races, it never made up for it. To have won Paris–Roubaix would have been worth more than all my other victories put together."

He left the peloton in 1990, still unhappy. "I was never respected in my own land because I rode for Dutchmen," he said.

He opened a bike company in Brecht, then closed it after five years because he couldn't stand working indoors. He began work in the building business and dreamed of building a small museum behind his house to show his bikes, jerseys and trophies.

Jan Raas on the other hand won the world road championship, ten stages of the Tour de France and five Amstel Gold races.

The 1984 race went to John Kelly. That's not what the records say but John is Sean Kelly's real name. His father was called John and so the son would be, too. But that would confuse everyone and so he was immediately referred to as Sean. Had his family realized what their son would do, and where, they would probably have stuck with John. Pronouncing Sean as *Shawn* was beyond foreign television commentators. He became instead See-yann Kelly.

John James "See-yann" Kelly was born to live in a scrappy farmhouse of a tin-roofed cottage at Curraghduff, to the south of Carrick-on-Suir. It's 165 kilometers from Dublin, the Irish capital, but that's by distance. Emotionally, Dublin is another world. Carrick-on-Suir, population 5,906, among other things home of a club for lovers of diesel railway locomotives, is plenty big enough. And Kelly is big enough to Carrick that he features on the town's website, which says: "Sean Kelly was consistently one of the top achievers in professional cycling for over 18 years. With his 22 classics wins he is statistically the fourth most successful cyclist of all time behind Eddy Merckx (50), Bernard Hinault (29) and Jacques Anquetil (29)."

It may never have happened had the family's 45 acres been enough to support another adult. But they couldn't, and so at 14 Kelly became a bricklayer, with enough money to buy a bike to ride with the local club.

The town has named its gym and swimming pool after him. And also a square in the town, or at any rate a widened area of Greystone Street between Kehoe's bar and a cash-and-carry. It prompted Kelly to say that in Ireland such things usually happened only when you're dead—a short quip from a man so famous for lack of words that rumor insisted he once nodded to a question during a radio interview.

Kelly was the first English-speaker to win Paris–Roubaix. He was living then with a cycling couple, Herman and Elise Nys at Vilvoorde, near Brussels. Kelly was proud of his filthy bike and left it upside down the garage so that journalists could admire it and he could revel in his glory. That sounds romantic. But that wasn't Kelly. Two days later the novelty had worn off and the journalists were no longer arriving. Kelly had other races to ride. He cursed that he now had to clean the bike himself when he could have left it to a team mechanic in Roubaix.

The rider the fans really wanted to see in Kelly's race was the man who'd won in 1978, 1979 and 1980. They'd never have given Francesco Moser a hope of winning again had the news not broken that January that he had not only broken Eddy Merckx's hour record but, after four days' rest, had gone back and ridden even further. Moser had been prepared by a "miracle" doctor, Francesco Conconi, but to the crowd's disappointment that preparation didn't include riding Paris–Roubaix.

On the other hand, Kelly's preparation hadn't gone well, either. Or at any rate not perfectly. On top of that, his team sponsors were repeatedly changing. Until 1978 he had ridden for Flandria, the Belgian bike factory, a precarious team with a long list of subsidiary sponsors who hadn't lasted the course. The factory was run by Aimé Claeys, whose meeting in a café with Léon van Daele had brought the team about. Claeys' partner was his brother, Rémi. The two argued so bitterly that they built a wall down the middle of their factory at Zedelgem and Aimé ran one end and Rémi the other. Aimé kept the Flandria name and Rémi tried to snub him by making better bikes he pointedly named Superia.

Superia, too, had a team and it was this for which Kelly rode in 1979, 1980 and 1981.

The complications had merely started. In 1978 it turned out that another Claeys, this time Pol, had built a nightclub called the Flandria Ranch without planning permission and on farming land outside the town of Torhout. It burned down. Pol Claeys was nothing if not an original thinker. In 1974 he had the idea of running not just one but two teams. One would continue to be in Belgium and the other would be in France, based around Cyrille Guimard, a sprinter who came close to winning the Tour de France.

Claeys registered his team in France as Merlin Plage-Shimano-Flandria, its main sponsor a property developer which for much of the 1970s was a sizable backer of the Tour de France. He then registered his other team in Belgium: Carpenter-Confortlux-Flandria. Both would ride Flandria bikes and have the name on their jerseys

To get round rules that a sponsor couldn't have more than one team, Flandria in Belgium was presented as a sewing machine company. Flandria did indeed make sewing machines, along with light motorcycles. The ploy worked. For a moment. Then fellow sponsors objected, aware that whatever the niceties, Flandria had built a team far larger than theirs. Two teams with one sponsor equaled, for them, one large team. But the Belgian federation stood firm. Frustrated, the sponsors called on teams in France to boycott races which Merlin-Flandria entered. GAN, Peugeot, Bic and Sonolor all stayed away from Milan–San Remo—but both Flandria teams took part.

Only cycling could find the compromise that followed: the French allowed the French Merlin-Flandria to ride Paris–Roubaix in 1974 provided it covered the Flandria name on its jerseys. In return, the Belgian team could ride the Tour de France if it too covered Flandria's name. Nobody thought to insist the names were painted out on the bikes as well. So Flandria still got the publicity it had set out to acquire.

Flandria went into receivership in 1981. By then the sponsorship problem had ended, the French team going its own way along with its manager, Jean de Gribaldy, the man who had discovered Kelly. And the Irishman went back to him, under the colors of Sem-France Loire, in 1982.

Sem in 1984 became a secondary sponsor to Skil, a maker of power tools. Skil paid a lot for Kelly and the pressure in 1984 was mounting. He had to justify not only his salary but the loyalty of riders. When he came second in Milan–San Remo and the Ronde van Vlaanderen, he promised he'd do better in Paris–Roubaix.

His biggest obstacle came from Holland, from Panasonic, the sponsor which had taken over the Raleigh team. Peter Post drilled them just as tightly. Further threats came from Laurent Fignon and Greg LeMond. With so many stars in the race, nobody expected that a track pursuiter, the stylish Alain Bondue, would be leading by almost a minute and a half by Arenberg. The crowd at the track bubbled with excitement: Bondue was born in Roubaix. On his wheel was a German, Gregor Braun, another track rider, winner of the pursuit at the Montreal Olympics in 1976. Both rode for La Redoute, a team sponsored by a mail-order company with its headquarters in the town.

"All we'd planned to do was be in front at the Arenberg," Bondue said afterwards. The race had struck him as dangerous as riders banged shoulders and elbows to keep their place in the lead. "When I looked round, the only person with me was Braun. We had 80 seconds when we got back on to the surfaced road and we felt good, but there were still a hundred kilometers to go…" They pressed on, Bondue with a sweat band round his forehead, Braun wearing a cloth cap turned backwards.

They made an improbable breakaway—but a worrying one because two pursuiters with a minute and 20 seconds aren't a safe proposition to anyone else with ambition. And the two men knew each other well because as as well and being teammates on the road, they had been a pairing in the Paris six-day. Kelly sat back and watched. Two other teams—Quantum and Splendor—had taken on the chase and the pursuiters were riding alone into a headwind. He could bide his time.

Then Braun began to struggle. And then he flatted. Bondue waited and they set off once more. They hadn't lost much time but news of their vulnerability came back to the eight chasers. There were 46 kilometers to go. It was time to react. Kelly attacked so unexpectedly and with such a ferocity that only Rudy Rogiers, the Belgian who'd come second in the world amateur road championship in 1981, could reach him. They went past Bondue and Braun. Bondue clung to them but he fell so hard on the last but one stretch of cobbles that it took a minute to pick himself off the ground. His first fear was that he had broken his pelvis.

A Belgian spectator sorted out his bike and helped Bondue back in the saddle. The Frenchman gained a minute on Kelly and Rogiers but he was still 36 seconds behind at the end. On his 25th birthday he had led and then come that close to winning Paris–Roubaix.

That Kelly outsprinted Rogiers for that victory instead was no surprise. Rogiers had come second in the amateur version of the race in 1982, but he was a weak sprinter and easily overawed. He took such stage fright at the end of the world amateur championship in Prague in 1981 that he let Andrej Vedernikov ride away from him. The Russian had time to throw both arms in the air as Rogiers trailed behind. Since Belgians are the butt of jokes across Europe for supposed slow thinking, Rogiers was greeted next morning by headlines saying he had "forgotten" to sprint.

But he wasn't alone in being overawed. The next year's winner of Paris–Roubaix, Marc Madiot, said in an interview: "I had so much respect for the past that in 1983, when I found myself in the lead in Paris–Roubaix with Moser, De Vlaeminck and Kuiper, I didn't dare share the pace-making with them for fear of knocking them off."

Marc Madiot now is a hyper-tense team manager, a man who lives on his nerves and rarely lacks a cynical turn of phrase. In Paris–Roubaix in 1985 he was the outsider, even though he had won the amateur event in 1979. Moser had had his moment of glory—a long moment because he was clear alone for half an hour until a wheel jammed between cobbles and brought his run to an end—and minor attacks followed when he was caught. But it was with 15 kilometers to go that Madiot broke away in a group of eight. Then as the leaders bounced towards the bar at the Carrefour de l'Arbre, he left them where Hennie Kuiper had left them to win in 1983—and where he himself had broken away to win the amateur event six years earlier in 1979.

"I was feeling good 30 kilometers before we got to Roubaix," he said, "and I got to the cobbles ahead of the others and I sensed I was going to win. By the Carrefour de l'Arbre I felt even better and I could hear people shouting my name. That was wonderful but I had to keep concentrating on what I was doing." Had Franco Ballerini not been there then Madiot might not have attacked so hard: "I was scared of his sprint and I had to get rid of him," he said. Ballerini tried to stay with him but couldn't. Madiot reached the track almost two minutes ahead of his Renault teammate, Bruno Wojtinek.

Wojtinek isn't a name to conjure memories, even though he disposed of Kelly, Rudy Dhaenens, Eddy Planckaert and Greg LeMond by 12 seconds. He's not better known despite this early talent—he was only 22—because in 1989 he was riding to see his team manager, Jean-René Bernaudeau, when an accident with a car wrecked his right knee. He took up running a clothing store in Lille.

Dhaenens, who came fifth—he came second in 1986—died aged 36 in 1998 when his car crashed on the way to the finish of the Ronde van Vlaanderen. He was to have commentated on the Eurosport television channel. He crashed on the E40 main highway and died in hospital a day later.

These bloodied and battered warriors struggle through the rain, the cold, the mud, on roads better suited to ox carts than bicycles. But for the victor there is glory, immortality and a place in history among the giants of the road. Since 1896, the greatest bike racers on earth have come to test their very souls in this brutal and beautiful spectacle.

—John Tesh, CBS Sports, 1987

14

Tradition and Scandal

Think back and you'll remember that old Roubaix had its workers' quarter, along with the mill run by Maurice Perez and Théodore Vienne. They were the men who founded Paris–Roubaix and built the track on which it finished. Their factory was just off the avenue de la fosse aux Chênes. The avenue runs perhaps only 400 meters, from the junction of the rue du Collège in the north to where it ends, between an office block on one side and a line of apartments on the other, at the avenue des Nations-Unies.

It's a junction like any other and you'd never give it a thought were it not for two things: first the proximity to the Perez-Vienne mill and second the fact that in 1986 the race they inspired finished on the road there for the first time since 1942. And why was it there? Because the avenue des Nations-Unies passed the offices of La Redoute, the clothing mail-order company which had taken on sponsorship of the race.

La Redoute's links with Roubaix were undeniable. It belonged to the Perez and Vienne era, making clothes from local wool as early as 1875. It was 21 years older than the race it was taking on. It had sponsored a professional team from 1979 to 1985—Bondue and Braun's team—and now that it had dropped that, it was staying in cycling by supporting Paris–Roubaix. It was a logical decision given a quirk in French law which forbade mail-order companies to advertise by more normal means, a way to protect small business in the town centers that France holds so dear. What in America would be called Main Street mom-and-pop stores.

But the upset was considerable. Paris–Roubaix was a race of myth and tradition, of drama and color. To finish on a soulless road through a city center was efficient, but that's all it was. And efficiency wasn't a word associated with gods riding cobbles through rain and wind. The three-year stay on the avenue des Nations-Unies wasn't a happy one. The organizers accepted it because La Redoute was offering so much money, but they repeatedly appealed to the company's directors to respect tradition and spectacle.

Among those who complained was Jean-Marie Leblanc, later organizer of the Tour de France but then still a journalist for *L'Équipe*. "Couldn't we just whisper in their ears that the track isn't the old anachronism that it's said to be? And anyway, there's nothing to prevent La Redoute making it a happy promotional operation by giving the public a free spectacle."

In the end it was the image not only of Paris–Roubaix but also of La Redoute which ended the company's sponsorship. For centuries La Redoute had concentrated on the popular masses, the traditional market for catalog sales. It was a market allied to cycling, the workman's sport, the sport which had brought working men in their masses to Vienne and Perez's new track. La Redoute had become the biggest *vente-à-distance* company in France and the third biggest in the world. It stressed its quick delivery and dynamic approach by rewarding its riders who did well in time-trials, especially in the Tour de France.

But times were changing. The internet threatened traditional printed catalogs. La Redoute itself became a branch of Pinault, one of France's biggest groups. The time had come to move out of clothes for the masses and to concentrate on the more socially elite.

"There is now a gap between the image that the company wanted to give when it began to sponsor cycling and the the objectives of the group to which La Redoute belongs," wrote Karl Joly in his history of the race. Pinault saw its sports sponsorship on a snootier level, backing an ocean-going yacht.

La Redoute persisted with the race for a little longer, allowing it to return to the track. Word said that its heart was no longer in it, but that it worried that the moment it gave it up, any rival in the Nord region could take one of the year's and certainly northern France's biggest media occasions.

As for La Redoute's team, it could no longer afford it even had it wanted to. It was taken over by RMO (*Relation Main Ouevre*), which supplied temporary workers to whoever needed them. It was for RMO that Marc Madiot won. In the end, RMO couldn't afford it either. The team limped on from 1986 to the end of 1992 and then collapsed when the sponsor could no longer pay the salaries.

The first man to win outside La Redoute's offices was Sean Kelly. There was no grudge match with Madiot because the Frenchman was injured and couldn't ride. And the biggest names had started staying away: Bernard Hinault, Laurent Fignon, Hennie Kuiper, Stephen Roche. The result was a race of boring uncertainty, nobody confident enough to make a move. The race went through the Arenberg forest, split up, then regrouped. In the end, an hour from the finish, Moser grew bored and attacked. Four dozen riders stretched out on his wheel.

It was from them that Dhaenens tried his hand. Moser went after him, alarmed at this *lèse-majesté*, and so did Kelly. The group reassembled. The cobbles of Camphin-en-Pévèle indicated 18 kilometers to go. Kelly picked up speed. And the uncertainty that riddled the race struck again. Moser didn't go with him and nor did the long-haired Dutchman, Johan van der Velde. Instead, Kelly was followed by lesser lights: Dhaenens, Adri van de Poel and Ferdi van den Haute, who finished in that order behind him.

It was a fine and gloriously muddy race. But the lack of luster made it appropriate for a finish alone on an inner city road of showrooms and offices.

Kelly's luck didn't hold. He got as far as the Ennevlin cobbles in 1987 when he snapped his handlebars. He reached the same point in 1988 and broke his frame, going flying when his front wheel dropped out. He still managed to finish 16th, on a spare bike and with blood running down his face. He must have hoped for a good wash: the showers at Roubaix track are notoriously old-fashioned that many riders drop out, take a short cut to the finish and use the shower, so there's sometimes no hot water left when the race arrives.

Kelly's win on the avenue des Nations-Unies was in a less than dramatic race but it was positively eventful compared to 1988. This time the race started with an *échappée matinale*, a morning break allowed a couple of hours of riding ahead of the race to give lesser lights a chance to show the advertising on their jerseys to the TV cameras. It inconveniences nobody, it offers a moment of glory to humble foot soldiers and it helps negotiate another year's contract in a sport aware that everyone is trying to make a living.

And so the earth didn't tremble when Thierry Casas broke away, a Parisian who until then had won a couple of races nobody had heard of and come second in 1983 in Paris–Troyes. Paris–Roubaix had been going less than an hour. A dozen others went with him, largely as anonymous as Casas, and nobody took much notice. They had four and a half minutes after less than 10 kilometers.

The usual punctures and mishaps thinned out the break but there were still seven left when they left the Arenberg forest. Two more vanished and so the number came down. The bunch began to worry. Guido Tempi got to within 2 minutes 50 seconds with what was left of the rest 25 seconds behind him. Laurent Fignon and Bruno Wojtinek had their own bouts of chasing. But by now the supposed no-hopers at the front had the idea of winning and, instead of just matching the speed of the chasers, they picked up the pace.

Just two men had survived at the front by the exit from the Carrefour de l'Arbre: Thomas Wegmuller and Dirk Demol. It was a turn-up for Demol. José De Cauwer, his manager in the ADR team, had come close to dropping him. But it was a small team and its leader, Eddy Planckaert, had just won the Ronde van Vlaanderen and De Cauwer needed riders to sacrifice their bodies and chances for their leader. "I was one of the two guys supposed to cover breaks," he said. Instead he was in the break. "I was told by De Cauwer to go with the morning break. I was working for Eddy and waiting for him to come up. But at the back, nobody was working. So I told myself 'Stay in front—you're not a bad sprinter and you never know.'"

If Demol hadn't had enough good luck, more was to come. Wegmuller ran over a plastic bag as he rode through Roubaix and it jammed in his derailleur. The mechanic in the team car tugged it clear but still the gears still wouldn't work. He was now trapped. He could stay on his bike and hope that chance might help—Demol could puncture or a dog might knock him off—or he could get a bike with gears that worked but lose so much time in changing from one to the other that he could never re-catch Demol.

Wegmuller pushed on on his damaged bike, Demol behind him like a vulture, watching to see if his rival's gears started working. They didn't and Wegmuller could do no more than watch as Demol rode past him to win. Other than criteriums, it was the only professional race he had won. He retired after 1995, managed an amateur team in Belgium and then in 2000 became the assistant director of the Radioshack professional team.

Wegmuller, who came second but whom Demol said was in super shape that day, was no more illustrious. He had won barely anything before that day. He stopped racing at the end of 1994 and since 1995 he has been running a cycle-touring business in Cyprus.

And Thierry Casas, who started it all? He came in 67th, 14 minutes later, best and only finisher of his Caja Rural team.

Things got little better in 1989. Eddy Merckx had retired, Roger De Vlaeminck had stopped racing five years earlier, Sean Kelly was 32. Stephen Roche and others abandoned after a mass crash at the entrance to the Arenberg forest.

The winning break went at 60 kilometers. Eddy Planckaert was there, Dirk Dewolf, Jean-Marie Wampers and Gilbert Duclos-Lasalle. Edwig van Hooydonck and Marc Madiot joined them two kilometers later. Dewolf rode away from them 17 kilometers from the finish and only Wampers closed on him. They rode the last 9 kilometers together, Dewolf entering the track first and Wampers sprinting round him.

"When I saw the red triangle for the last kilometer, I thought of Gent–Wevelgem in 1986," he said. There he had blundered tactically and been beaten in a four-man break by Guido Bontempi and the Dutchman, Twan Poels.

"I was leading [in Paris–Roubaix] but what was going to happen at the finish? On top of that, that year there was the entrance into the track, a lot more impressive than finishing on the road [the avenue des Nations-Unies]. I got to the cement of the track and it was the whole spirit of Paris–Roubaix. I'd watched videos of races that had finished there before and I knew what mistakes I had to avoid. De Wolf rode just like I hoped he would. In the end, I don't know how much I beat him by. If I was in his place, I'd have wept. But that's life, isn't it?"

Wampers? He was, as Pascal Sergent put it, "scarcely known to the public." He was a jobbing Belgian professional, a stage winner in the Four Days of Dunkirk but with little else to his name. Peter Post had taken him into the Panasonic team as a domestique, a work-donkey, only to have him lose much of a year through mononucleosis—glandular fever. It left him so weak that he felt embarrassed to wear his jersey when he couldn't keep up with everyday *trimmers*, keep-fit cyclists, on Sunday mornings. And his miseries hadn't started there because his former team, Hitachi, was so cross at Wampers' plan to cross the border into Holland and race for Panasonic that it excluded him from big races for the rest of his contract.

Post's faith was repaid. Paris–Roubaix marked a turning for Wampers. In the same year, he won the Scheldeprijs (also known as the GP d'Escaut) in Belgium and the Grand Prix of Frankfurt (also known as the Henninger Turm) in Germany. He never had another season like it and faded into obscurity to retire after 1992.

The race is all about surviving, surviving, surviving.
I know I didn't feel great but maybe others felt worse.

—Tom Boonen, 2009

15

It Takes a Special Man, It Takes a Special Mount

Paris–Roubaix is a graveyard of ambitions. It can be a cemetery for bikes.

The first riders had little choice over what they rode. Not because, as now, their sponsor insisted but because there was nothing else. There was as much a difference between a race bike and a street bike as there is now, but the tubes, the welding, the wheels and the tires were heavier and more solid. That was the era when men rode alone. The Tour de France insisted they race through the night and demanded they repair their own bikes. The story of Eugène Christophe welding his fork together in a forge at the foot of the Tourmalet is the core of cycling legend.

Factories could doubtless make their bikes lighter, but what was the point if they failed on a rough road or a mountain track and cost their rider the race?

That's not to say the old guys didn't experiment. They used wooden rims even though metal was more common. It was lighter and it flexed more over bad roads, the wood being glued in strips rather than solid. The American bike historian, Sheldon Brown, said: "In many ways, wood is an ideal material for bicycle rims and most bicycles in the early part of the century were equipped with them. They are light, strong and resilient."

They had their problems, of course. They were little suited to rim brakes—the first brakes pushed down on the tire rather than squeeze the rim—because the wood wore too quickly. Riders got round that by using brake blocks of leather. They didn't last long but they were cheaper and easier to replace than a rim.

You had to know what you were doing when you built a wooden wheel because tightening the spokes too far could shatter the rim. Worse, the wheel might stand up in the workshop but a collision on the road could reduce it to splinters. A metal rim may go out of true but it would at least hold the rider upright.

It was because of the danger that wooden rims were eventually banned in road races. You can still get them, by the way. At least one company in Italy still makes them, which is appropriate because as late as 1938 Gino Bartali won the Tour de France on wooden rims. For a long time, Henri Desgrange banned metal rims in the Tour because he feared they would overheat in prolonged braking in the mountains and melt the glue with which the tires were held in place. Paris–Roubaix riders persisted with them for several years after world war two but a ban because of their fragility, and a difficulty in buying them anyway, led to their disappearance.

André Mahé recalled: "We rode the same bikes as the rest of the season. We didn't need to change them because they were much less rigid than modern bikes. The frames moved all over the place. When I attacked, I could feel the bottom bracket swaying underneath me." That was 1952.

Little changed for several decades beyond the normal improvement in bicycles. Riders softened their tires and if they could they used a frame with more than usual space for the wheels.

"With a normal frame you can do Paris–Roubaix but it has to be dry," says Julien Devriese, a tubby, round-faced, bespectacled former mechanic to Merckx, LeMond and Lance Armstrong. "When you come in the rain and then the mud, it all fills up. When you put your heavier tubulars in, they pass just [without rubbing the frame]. But when you have a rainy day on the mud on the road…" He waved his hand to demonstrate a bike slowing down.

In earlier days that wasn't a problem. Wheelbases were longer, angles softer and clearances larger. They needed to be because a shallower, longer bike with a greater curve in the front fork rode better over the rougher roads of the period. There is an irony that, for all that bikes have become nippier since then, and for all that bicycles of the 1950s and 1960s are now considered dinosaurs, modern riders still prefer a bike with a longer wheelbase to go over the cobbles.

Francesco Moser padded his handlebars with sponge beneath the conventional tape in the 1970s, but it wasn't until the 1990s that anything significant happened. It was then that Gilbert Duclos-Lasalle won Paris–Roubaix with suspended front forks. An American company, RockShox, promoted them amid sneers at European cycling being too traditional, too stubborn, to unimaginative to have adopted their ideas earlier. A flurry of riders fitted them, including LeMond. Not all were impressed.

RockShox's origins were in motorcycle racing, particularly cross-country moto-cross. The transfer to cycling seemed obvious and the first experiment, in downhill racing on tracks, was rewarding: Greg Herbold was the first downhill world champion as a test rider. The mountain bike boom came at a perfect time and the link with the cobbles of Paris–Roubaix was clear. Paul Turner, the company's founder, tried for two years to get a way in. The breakthrough came at a round-the-houses race in the south of France. Duclos-Lasalle was interested in the suspension of a mountain bike ridden by a marketing man called François Bourret. Bourret suggested suspended front forks could be perfect for races such as Paris–Roubaix. Duclos-Lasalle was interested but had to discuss it with his manager in the Z team, Roger Legeay.

Legeay, often considered a traditionalist, gave Duclos-Lasalle his agreement but insisted that the team's leader, Greg LeMond, had a pair as well. For RockShox it was an offer beyond its dreams. The company had six weeks to make a fork that would work.

The writer Zapata Espinoza said: "RockShox headed to Europe with two forks, one each for Duclos-Lasalle and LeMond, and enough spare parts to keep them working. As soon as the other Team Z riders saw the benefits of suspension over cobbles, they wanted them too. On the Thursday before the race Paul [Turner] called America to get more fork parts shipped—fast! The next day two steerer tubes were delivered at Charles de Gaulle airport for the small price of $600 [then a considerable sum].

"When the 1991 race came to a close, Gilbert was the top RockShox rider, in 12th place. It was an admirable showing and Duclos-Lasalle was so convinced that he vowed to win with suspension in '92."

The first experiment, though, produced raised eyebrows in the peloton but no interest. RockShox would have abandoned the experiment then—the road forks hadn't been put on sale—had Duclos-Lasalle not wanted to continue. And continue, it has to be said, in opposition to team mechanics across the sport who accused the Americans of meddling with a sport they didn't understand and with a technology that merely replaced something simpler and infallible that already worked.

Duclos-Lasalle did win in 1992 but the luster didn't last. The Australian, Stuart O'Grady, said: "When I first rode Paris–Roubaix, I didn't really have a lot of choice but to use them. They were heavy and the

Gilbert Duclos-Lasalle put his RockShox forks to the test on the cobbles. of Paris–Roubaix

advantage you got over the cobbles was marginal. When you got on to the normal Tarmac it was like riding in quicksand. All your energy went into turning these little nuts to tighten the pressure on the forks— and you couldn't feel your fingers. That was a total nightmare, so I was happy to go back to a normal bike."

Devriese's comment: "When you have too many things on a bike you lose a lot of power. The thing with [RockShox forks], when you put this on a rider's bike and he's happy with it, he forgets his back wheel and he's crashing all of the holes and all the flat tires were in the back."

Very little is ever new in cycling. Disc wheels were first made in 1891. Frames made entirely of aluminum appeared in 1894. And a bicycle with suspension was among the prizes for the first road race in 1869. RockShox had simply reinvented, although doubtless improved, what had existed for 125 years: and been dismissed for just as long. Suspension returns every so often, only to vanish again.

If riders prefer to take a hammering rather than use suspension, there has to be a good reason, for Paris–Roubaix is a shatterer of men. O'Grady: "You can't understand from the TV or photos how hard it is. Paris–Roubaix is the only race I get my wrists taped for. And my fingers. There's tape on my hips for *when* I crash, too, not *if*. It's like getting ready for a boxing match.

"The faster you go, the easier it is. The problem is that the more tired you get, the slower you get—so the harder they become. The best way is to ride straight down the middle of the road. It's the hardest but it's the best. When riders start getting a bit tired or a bit desperate they dive off into the side or into the dirt because it's a little bit easier to ride there, but that's where the rocks end up and when all the punctures are going to happen.

"The guys riding down the center of the road are generally the guys who are going pretty strongly. There's just so much emphasis on position coming into the cobbles. If you aren't in the first 10 you're really asking for trouble. Every water bottle becomes a land mine. There are bottles going everywhere and spilling water, so a lot of it is just about getting a good position at the start."

The falls are still frequent but flat tires get fewer each year. Paris–Roubaix and particularly the Arenberg is trickier than the Ronde van Vlaanderen, Tom Boonen says. In general, he said, "there is always a line to follow and you fix yourself on it to avoid a crash. But on the Arenberg there is nothing to follow and the holes are everywhere. And contrary to the Koppenberg in the Ronde van Vlaanderen, which is preceded by the Kwaremont and the Patersberg, which calm the spirit a bit, you get to the Arenberg at a crazy speed."

Riders may fall but their bikes break less often. "We changed about 20 wheels today," said the Mavic mechanic Yves Hézard, himself a former professional, in 2001. The French accessories company provides spare wheels and bikes from yellow cars and motorbikes that follow the race. "Every year we change fewer, because the wheels and tires are getting better and better. Five years ago it was much worse. We'd be changing about a hundred. So, yes, our job is easier—except that the race generally goes faster now, so we're under a bit more pressure.

"Every year there are new types of gears, new aluminum frames, new titanium frames, so it's getting more complex for us and becoming more and more difficult to offer neutral assistance. We have a list in the car of who is riding Mavic or Shimano or Campagnolo. The moment someone gets a flat, we need to think of a lot of things at once. Is it a titanium frame or a carbon frame or a steel frame? It's nerve-wracking."

The choice of carbon, titanium and other frames is important to mechanics because the wheel slots differ in width. The wheel fixing can be adjusted beside the road and it takes only seconds but the mechanic is under pressure and riders under stress. The choice of Mavic, Shimano and Campagnolo is also significant because patent disputes mean the sprockets on one company's wheels may not work with another factory's gears. None of this mattered in the years before gears were indexed and operated by small switches behind the brake levers. Riders reached down to a lever on the side of his bike, or sometimes at the end of the handlebars, and moved it one way or the other until he heard and felt the chain engage properly on the next cog. All that has changed, not least because riders no longer have to sit down to change gear.

Most riders used Campagnolo equipment until Shimano's arrival in the peloton in 1973. A few teams, mainly French, used Simplex gears but even then everything was compatible. Such was the passion of some fans that they'd take their own wheels to the roadside in the hope of helping a rider in need. And, because it was a tradition, in the hope of getting a brand new wheel from his team in thanks. Since then, teams have relied on their own cars of spares, on the neutral help offered by Mavic, and on friends and relatives stationed along the road in difficult sites where cars and motorbikes have trouble passing.

Riders, as O'Grady observed, don't always choose what they ride. They are tied by their teams' contracts with suppliers. It is sport but it is just as much advertising. A bike that snaps is bad news. Not just for the rider but for the people who made the bike. Paris–Roubaix is a smaller version of what Formula 1 racing represents for makers of car tires: a way to impress a wider public with lightweight but rugged dependability.

The French company, Time, is in permanent battle with its counterpart, Look. The marketing people of both seek the advantage. Look soaked up the pedal market so Time, which also makes pedals, decided to go instead for carbon front forks. Eleven of the 22 teams in the 1997 Tour de France used Time forks. That established their lightness. The following year Time picked on Paris–Roubaix to overcome suspicions that carbon forks were brittle and show they could stand up to the worst.

Carbon had been around since experiments by Raleigh's special products division, as it was called with pompous secrecy, in 1972. Nobody could enter the offices without a security pass. Special Products, in fact, was what remained of the Carlton Cycles company where the chance meeting with Lord Plowden brought about Peter Post's TI-Raleigh team. Its problem was its enormous cost, the inevitable pessimistic predictions about anything that was neither steel nor aluminum, and its rigidity.

Time's forks were almost a kilo lighter than forks with suspension. They were simpler to fit, easier to maintain. But they were greeted with suspicion. Armel André, who worked with riders such as Richard Virenque and Alex Zülle at Festina, was dubious. "It may be lighter," he said, "but it makes no difference to a rider's comfort. It doesn't absorb energy or vibration better than any other material. That's what your elbows do. That's where the shocks are absorbed."

He changed only reluctantly from steel and aluminum. Carbon forks, which can't be bent into the traditional curve like steel or aluminum, *looked* more rigid whether they were or not. But within a few seasons, Time's bet had succeeded. As the writer Michel Dalloni said in *Le Figaro*, the heavyweight French daily, "the day that Frédéric Moncassin dominated on Time forks at the exit from the Hell of the North, those who followed (and his fans among everyday cyclists) demanded carbon for themselves. That's not the least merit of Paris–Roubaix."

Crazy thing—I dislocated my finger and somehow it popped back into place before I got to the finish.

—Michael Barry, 2011

16

Bouncing Back to Victory

Three French wins in a row was more than the home nation could expect. Especially when the first, by Marc Madiot in 1991, came from a man dismissed as a has-been because of problems with his health.

But more surprising still were Gilbert Duclos-Lasalle's wins in 1992 and again in 1993. "Gibus", as Duclos-Lasalle was known, was no youngster. In 1992 he was 37. Few continued to race at that age. Still fewer were given any hope.

Duclos-Lasalle rode his suspension forks in 1991 and came 12th. He fitted them again in 1992 and attacked with 40 kilometers left to ride. He had led the bunch coming out of the Arenberg forest, just Jean-Paul van Poppel, and Rik van Slycke behind him. Greg LeMond was keeping the pace down in the bunch for his team leader.

Duclos' problem was that his companions were sprinters. There was a chance he could master van Slycke but van Poppel was a class above above him, a man who won 94 races as a professional, 22 of them stages in big stage races. He had no choice but to drive them into the ground. He recalled a tactic which De Vlaeminck and Didi Thurau had pulled on him 12 years earlier when everyone had jumped him at Ennevelin and he never caught them. If it worked for them, it could work for him. And it did. He dropped them and won by 34 seconds, not over his breakaway companions, who were swallowed by the bunch, but over the German, Olaf Ludwig, who had set off in lone chase.

In 1993 he did it again. He punctured as he led at the start of the first stretch of cobbles. The glory that came with leading was that the mechanics were behind everyone else. He had to wait for everyone to pass before he could change his wheel. The wheel held up fine but he didn't—500 meters later he crashed.

"I had only one teammate when I started chasing," he said. "I didn't see how I would get back on." But he did. He wiggled through the stragglers and then the field. He left them all and reached the track with just a young Italian, Franco Ballerini—and won Paris–Roubaix for the second successive year.

Ballerini was disgusted. He thought he'd won. He'd chased Duclos along the finish straight and, so far as he was concerned, had bettered him by the width of a tire. Riders usually know these things better than the judges. Sometimes they influence them by throwing an arm in the air, as Ballerini did. But Ballerini genuinely thought he'd won. And so did the judges. Who announced the Italian as winner.

But then doubt and technology set in. Officials crowded round the photo-finish machine as it printed its picture. And they saw that both they and Ballerini had been wrong. It needed a photo to separate them, but Duclos-Lasalle, on the inside of the track, had won by eight centimeters. Ballerini had been the faster but he had passed Duclos only *after* the line.

"I'm never going to ride a bike again," Ballerini mumbled angrily, hiding his head in the track center. "What a swindle. Everything was perfect. I was so strong."

He did ride again, of course, and he won Paris–Roubaix in 1995 and 1998. But life held a greater tragedy than his defeat by Duclos-Lasalle. He retired in 2001 and became team selector for the Italian federation. In his spare time he took up car rallying. In February 2010 he was the navigator in a car driven by Alessandro Ciardi during a rally at Larciano, in Tuscany. The Renault left the road on a bend at 100 kilometers per hour, bumped on to grass and hit the wall of a house. Ballerini died of his injuries shortly afterward.

Duclos-Lasalle's career ended after 19 professional seasons in 1995 after a hunting accident almost cost him a hand. He works now as an occasional presenter on television, where his raincoat and his life-saddened expression give him the air of a man who has once more missed the last bus home.

The man of the race in 1994 had the thighs of a sprinter and the grace of an elephant: Andreï Tchmil. He was Russian. Sometimes he smiled but mostly he made Leonid Brezhnev look like a party boy. Tchmil was born in Khabarovsk in 1963 and knew no other leader until Brezhnev died in 1982. *Procycling* said: "The harsh elements are his racing allies: the cold, the wind, the rain. His physique recalls the indestructible monuments of Soviet heavy industry: the welding is functional, the materials unyielding, the breaking strength unknown." And yet, bizarrely, he was the son of an opera singer and he enjoyed singing and listening to classical music.

Tchmil grew up 30 kilometers from China. Khabarovsk is a pretty city of perhaps half a million people, a strategic site in the Soviet Union's occasional spats with China but never closed to foreigners. Japanese leaders were tried there after using biological weapons in world war two.

Tchmil passed his childhood in the city before getting his first bike at 15 and leaving for a sports school in Gorki. There he applied for his first racing license in 1981. It was headed CCCP, Cyrillic initials of the Soviet Union.

In December 1991 the USSR separated into 15 states. Gorki was in Russia and the heading on Tchmil's license changed accordingly. But Gorki had never been home. That was Khabarovsk, in Moldova, and in 1993 and 1994 he held a Moldovan license. The problem was that Moldova wasn't recognized by the UCI. Another was that Moldova demanded Tchmil pay $5,000. He solved that by riding for Ukraine, which asked nothing, from 1994 to 1997.

He raced on that license when he moved to Belgium in 1998. He then took Belgian nationality, completing quite a collection of passports for just one man.

"People are cynical when I talk about Belgium," he said. "They think I'm only Belgian on paper. That's not true. Yes, I was Russian, even a proud one. Now I'm proud to be Belgian. The first thing I did was learn French."

Tchmil was the epitome of the uncompromising Russian. He used his thighs and calves to crash straight through cobbles and holes. If he smashed his bike, there was always another. Frank Vandenbroucke, who was in the Lotto team with him in 1994, said: "Tchmil came from some invisible Russian village near the Chinese border and he'd just transferred from GB-MG, where Museeuw, Ballerini and Cipollini rode. Two years before that he was with Alfa Lum, the only Russian team, with legendary hard men such as Abdoujaparov, Konichev and Ivanov, who'd ride right through a hill if they thought that was what it took."

Tchmil wasn't a worrier. "I don't think of things the same way as other riders," he said when a reporter asked if he hoped to copy De Vlaeminck and win the Ronde van Vlaanderen and Paris–Roubaix in the same season. "I only really start thinking about a race the day before. It's pointless worrying about it all the preceding week because come the Sunday and you're psychologically tired and you have to start the race getting over the nightmare of the previous week."

Tchmil must have been the only man not to have a waking nightmare that morning of Sunday, April 10, 1994—it was snowing. The

Andreï Tchmil, Paris–Roubaix 1994: don't worry, be happy

bunch was depressed and rode on doggedly. A Czech, Lubos Lum, headed off through the snow and picked up 14 minutes on all but Steffen Wesemann, a Swiss who had also gone off by himself. But Lum became glum. It had seemed a good idea to push off and show his jersey but by Solesmes the gloss had gone. Instead of grabbing a bag of food and riding on, he stopped by the roadside for a minute before continuing no more happy than he'd been before. The peloton caught him 15 kilometers later and with some relief he gave up.

Tchmil's moment came 20 kilometers after Orchies. He played the classic card of attacking when a breakaway was caught and opened 40 seconds. Crashes and flat tires hindered the chase and Tchmil won by 1 minute 13 seconds.

The crowd was as enthusiastic as anyone ever was about Tchmil. He was a local by then in as much as he lived in Roubaix during the winter. It had been French that he had learned rather than the Dutch of most Belgian riders. Ballerini came second and in 1996 finally won.

Tchmil raced for the last time in May 2002. By then his lack of identity troubled him. "I no longer feel that I belong to any nation," he said with sadness. He never felt Belgium accepted him, nor that any team valued him. He advised the Chocolat Jacques team in Belgium for a while but packed it in when, he said, the riders took no notice of him. He moved back to Moldova in August 2006 and became minister of sport.

Ten years before he went, in 1996, a single team not only provided the first three riders, they led the field in by more than two and a half minutes. And the team also provided the fifth placed rider. If Paris–Roubaix demanded something special for its centenary, it got it. Such an event was bettered only in 1910, when Alcyon took the first four places.

Johan Museeuw, Gianluca Bortolami, Andrea Tafi and Franco Ballerini in 1996 all rode for Mapei. What they were advertising was tiling glue. Rodolfo Squinzi, a young businessman from Milan, founded the company in 1937 with a staff of three. It expanded across the world to become one of the world's largest suppliers of adhesives and sealants to the building industry. By 1996 the company was being run by Rodolfo's son, Giorgio, and it was his wife who was often credited with designing the dazzle camouflage design of the team's jerseys.

Frank Vandenbroucke, who rode for the team, recalled a conversation in his family's bar in Belgium:

"All those colors mixed up together. Those Mapei-GB jerseys are a mess, aren't they?"

"I was told Squinzi's wife designed them."

"Who?"

"Squinzi, the boss of Mapei, a building company."

"I hope his buildings look better than his jerseys."

"Maybe that's why they win so much. They want to get to the finish as fast as they can to put something else on."

Mapei's domination of Paris–Roubaix, under its manager, Patrick Lefevère, placed the first three again in 1998—Ballerini, Tafi and Wilfried Peeters—and again in 1999: Tafi, Peeters, Tom Steels.

That Lefevère didn't just strike lucky with the riders he could contract with Mapei's money showed when, with Domo, he placed the first three in 2001—Servais Knaven, Museeuw and Romain Vainsteins—and then with Quick Step (a tiling company previously a co-sponsor with Mapei) won the race thanks to Tom Boonen in 2005, 2008 and 2009.

The odd man out among all his winners is Knaven: because he competes under a made-up name. His passport calls him Hendrikus Knaven, which is his real name. He came to be that because his father had had a few beers too many when he went to register the birth. When he got to the office, he couldn't remember what he and his wife had agreed to call their child. Worried that he'd look stupid in front of officialdom and others in the office—who forgets the name of his own child?—he blurted out "Hendrikus", the only name he could think of.

"He went back to the register office a little bit later but they told him it cost 200 guilders to change a first name," Servais-named-Hendrikus recounted. "That was a lot of money for my parents back then and so, officially, I have stayed Hendrikus even though I've always been called Servais."

And another odd story before the chapter ends:

The sign—the *panneau*—showing that just 10 kilometers remained in the 2006 race stood on the far side of a railway crossing a little after Chéreng. Measured the other way, it came after 249 kilometers, just beyond the last big stretch of cobbles at Gruson. Barriers striped in red and white stood vertically, pointing to the sky. Two pairs of rails ran at right angles to the road, the gap between them filled by concrete slabs.

The previous winter, messages had gone to all the mayors along the route and to SNCF, the national railway company, to say that the race was coming their way. The hope was that nothing would hinder the race. And for a while nothing did. Fabian Cancellara bumped across unhindered and rode on. It was a little after 5pm. Between Cancellara's lone passage and the arrival of the chasers, the crossing bell rang and, after a moment for drivers to take note, the red and white barriers began to descend across the road. Bright yellow lights pulsed. A freight train was about to pass.

Trains have always had priority over road traffic because they are hard to stop and because they run to interlocking timetables. A delay in one train delays many more and the consequences are worse for travelers and freight than the few minutes spent waiting at the roadside.

Claude Deschaseaux, the president of the race commissaires, could see the race on the television in his car. "The barrier was vertical when Cancellara passed," he said. "It went down when his chasers were still 80 meters away." The barriers crossed just the right hand side of the road in each direction. Beneath the road, a black box registered the moment each vehicle entered and left the crossing, a way of analyzing accidents that happen when drivers slalom round the barriers regardless.

And slalom was just what Leif Hoste, Peter van Petegem and Vladimir Gusev did. And they were disqualified. The UCI's rules left no choice. "Yes, certainly, we were in a critical moment of the race," Deschaseaux said. "And passion can get the better over judgment. But the rule is there and it doesn't give us latitude to interpret it. If you leave the door open to riders then one day one of them will be crushed by a train. And it's in the biggest races that we have to give a good example."

Van Petegem wasn't impressed: "When I saw the barrier come down, I slipped my foot out of the pedal. But when I saw Hoste ride through, I followed him by reflex. No one was in danger. You think that if Cancellara had done it, they would have disqualified *him*? It's crazy. In Belgium they would have stopped the train, but not here."

Hoste admitted: "I know what the rule says, yes. But I don't know why they didn't stop us [to re-establish the original advantage over Tom Boonen, Alessandro Ballan and Juan Antonio Flecha, who *had* stopped] nor why nobody said anything to us in the 10 kilometers that followed. All that just to hear that we'd been disqualified two minutes before we'd have gone on to the podium. Cancellara deserved his victory but, for me, in my thoughts, I was the man who came second to him even though I was disqualified."

The difference between Formula 1 car racing and cycling is that you can win a Grand Prix with dysentry—but you'll never win Paris–Roubaix with hemorrhoids.

—Laurent Ruquier, broadcaster

17

Of Scandal and Saving Children's Heads

In Roubaix's old shower block, the man from *Procycling* observed in 2001, "Lars Michaelsen steps unsteadily towards the cubicle where his bags and drink have been left awaiting his arrival by his team soigneur. He sits down and is immediately racked by a coughing fit brought on by the lungfuls of dust inhaled on the windswept pavé."

Somehow it sums it up. Can there be a race, anywhere in the world, over a course that no sane soul would use on a Sunday morning spin? Can there be a race which men enter knowing they stand no chance of winning, that they'll play little part in the victory, their own or their teammates', that there's nothing they can do to help their leader—and that so dreadful are the roads that men have broken legs, collar bones and come close to losing their lives?

And yet…well, as Fabian Cancellara put it: "It's amazing when you're alone in the final kilometers. Until you've won Paris–Roubaix, you can't imagine what it's like. By winning alone you show quality, you show strength. It's like a war and you're the last man standing."

So crushing was the Swiss rider's victory in 2010—when he rode away from the field with 49 kilometers to go—that rumor spread he had a motor on his bike. Since it's hard to hide a motor on a bike, the assumption was that it was in the bottom bracket, the bearing around which the pedals turn. And just such a motor had indeed been manufactured. The story started when an Italian, Michele Bufalino, produced such a bike and said: "I have tried to do everything to alert the cycling world to the existence and use of this motor in the world of cycling."

Davide Cassani, a former professional, demonstrated a bike fitted with a motor on RAI, the Italian television company where he worked as a consultant. The bike looked normal, said a reporter from the *New York Times*. But "when he pressed a button hidden under the rubber hood of a brake lever, the pedals began turning, powered by a motor and batteries tucked into its frame. Cassani, 49 and long retired, said the assistance of a motor might enable him to return to racing and win a stage of the Giro d'Italia, which ended Sunday. Such bicycles, he said, had been used by professional riders in races, but he offered no names."

Gruber, which makes the motor at its headquarters in Wörgl, a railroad junction northeast of Innsbruck in Austria, says the Assist feels "as if another person were pushing your bike from behind." It is powered by a battery in the frame and operated from a switch in the brake lever mounting.

Bufalino combined Cassani's demonstration with comments of his own and posted them on You Tube. He pointed to what he considered suspicious movements of Cancellara's hand and remarked on the speed and power of some of his accelerations. The story spread so fast that Gruber's website crashed.

Bufalino was unrepentant: "It has come to be seen as an attack on Cancellara," he said. "But I think the most important objective, which, remember, was to raise the question of this practice in high places in cycling, has been achieved. I never accused Cancellara. I invited everyone to reflect, and this has happened."

"I'm not even going to waste my time answering such a stupid allegation," was how Cancellara replied when newspapers questioned him in Switzerland. "I thought it was funny when I first heard it but the joke's worn thin now." And the sport's governing body, the UCI, said it doubted the story, trusted Cancellara's integrity but added that it would devise a test for the future. In the end the story died without anyone's mentioning Gruber's insistence that the motor could be fitted in a frame of steel or aluminum frame but not in carbon.

Cancellara, a multilingual, smiling and amusing man, had to get rid of Boonen in that Paris–Roubaix of 2010. He wouldn't win if he reached the track with him but, as the best solo rider in the bunch, he could gamble on staying clear if he could manage to escape. Boonen, of course, would do all he could to ensure that he didn't. Cancellara saw his moment when there were 49 kilometers to ride. Boonen was eating at the back of the group. Cancellara spotted it and attacked while the Belgian's mouth was full. He got 25 meters immediately.

Fabian Cancellara: so good they said he had a motor

Boonen was powerless. Demoralized, even, because he couldn't match Thor Hushovd, a Norwegian, and Juan Antonio Flecha, a Spaniard, when they went off in pursuit.

Cancellara in his red jersey with white cross of Swiss national champion, crossed the line with his arms raised, exactly two minutes ahead of the rest. He became the second Swiss to have won Paris–Roubaix and the Ronde van Vlaanderen in the same year, after Heiri Suter in 1923. Cancellara won Paris–Roubaix in 6 hours 35 minutes 10 seconds. That was close on two and three-quarters of an hour sooner than the first winner, Josef Fischer, who also won by two minutes.

But what of the cobbles he rode, the tracks, the roads that make the race, their future? What of these paths of champions?

The story of pavé—*kinderkopjes* or children's heads as they're known in Dutch—started with the industrial revolution in the second half of the 19th century. Farming was restructured at the same time and the two together demanded roads better than the mud tracks which was all most areas had. Most of the stones came from the Artois or from Hainaut, in Belgium. Some were brought further, from Brittany, others from nearer by. There were, for instance, more than 300 quarries in Louvigné-le-Désert, in northern France, by 1850 and twice as many 50 years later. Word had it that a skilled worker could make almost 150 cobbles a day if things went well. His whole day's output covered just a meter and a half of road.

The cobbles awarded to the winners aren't just hooked out of the ground. Bertrand Duhem, a stone worker from Orchies whose job it is to clean them for presentation, has as part of his contract to see that they were handmade, that they have been used on a road in the Nord, and that they are of local manufacture. He can identify a cobble and its origins just from looking.

"Let me see," he says, turning a stone in his hand, "that's not blue enough to be from Louvigné. No, beige like that, it must be from Languédias."

Some of these original roads still exist, or at least fragments do. They have survived time, weather and traffic. The stones lie still in neat patterns. Paris–Roubaix has never used them because they don't lead anywhere. Their ends have been sealed by plowing or by sinking land.

The future of Paris–Roubaix is more secure than for decades. Even if it ever started somewhere else, its finish is in Roubaix and therefore much of its cobbles are secure. Karl Joly says in his study of the race's position in the city: "The image of the town declined after the prosperity that came from the cloth industry…Roubaix is trying to attract new companies and residents through a youth policy that has created new universities and schools. It's in this context that Paris–Roubaix has become a communications tool for the city. It's a way of using the values of the race to attract new investors that could give a new élan to the commune."

He quoted the French rider, Gilbert Duclos-Lasalle, who remembered a teammate telling him that if he could get to the track before the gates closed then he could call himself a real racer. By extension, Joly said, "Because the race is the hardest there is, the winner achieves recognition from everyone. The commune of Roubaix wants to operate in the same way to attract new investors: investing in Roubaix is a bet which, at the finish, will prove a winner."

Roubaix pictures the race on advertising posters. A placard on the road that leads to the track reads "*Je Paris–Roubaix*", turning the name of the race into a verb—"I Paris–Roubaix" and, by extension, "therefore I triumph."

But it is not safe. There is still no decree to protect the cobbles as a national *patrimoine*. Only those through the Arenberg forest are safe because the road is private—it belongs to the Domaine des Eaux et Forêts—and local communes can't lay tar over it.

But the rest are as vulnerable as any other road. As Pascal Sergent put it: "You have to realize that mayors are masters in their own domain and they face electoral pressure from voters who complain 'Look, I've had enough of those cobbles—they're ruining my car!'"

There is enough concern that in 1980 more than 10,000 people signed a petition that the cobbles and the route of Paris–Roubaix should be listed as a national treasure. An exhibition with that aim was held in Paris in 1982. The alarm had been sounded: "Pretty soon," said Alain Bernard, "the media and politicians joined our concern to preserve what we had."

Groups of enthusiasts, former riders, officials—anybody with an interest—merged in 1995 to form *Les Amis de Paris–Roubaix*. There are members all over France but also in Britain, Belgium, Holland, Luxembourg, Germany, Sweden, Italy, Canada and the USA. They provide a cobble for each year's winner. Roger De Vlaeminck was first, in 1977, before Les Amis were constituted. Sean Kelly has his embedded in the wall of his house, as has Andrea Tafi. They present them, too, to former winners.

The honor isn't taken lightly. When a frail André Mahé received his, in September 2006, the presentation was attended by 91-year-old Émile Masson, winner in 1939, who had come from his home in Liège.

In 2002, *Les Amis* gave a five-tonne cobble to the town of Roubaix. For some, though, time got there first. Maurice Garin's cobble was laid on his grave near Lens. Tradition, too, has named stretches of cobbles after riders who made them or the race noteworthy. The first honors Jean Stablinski at the entrance to the Arenberg forest. At Haveluy there's a memorial to Jean Donain, the founder of the GP de Denain, the North's other big race.

Then between Beuvry and Orchies are the Marc Madiot cobbles, followed by Gilbert Duclos-Lasalle's dedicated stretch between Cysoing and Boughelles and Hennie Kuiper's from Willemmes to Hem. Then finally come the Charles Crupelandt cobbles in Roubaix itself.

The race director, Jean-François Pescheux said of them:

Troisvilles: "It's the start of the hell. Rather than the cobbles themselves, it's above all the preceding kilometers that are impressive. The bunch is entirely silent. All you hear is the sound of brakes on rims. The riders become very nervous and waves set in across the peloton."

Haspres-Haveluy: "I'm always impressed on these two sectors by the toil of the team men to get their leaders into the best position before Arenberg. It's the first big *écrémage* [literally: creaming, meaning a destructive effort], the first violent push on the accelerator. The best 20 or 25 riders get to the front of the bunch. In the Mapei era, all the leaders were up front. The other half of the team had already ended their race."

Wandignies-Orchies: "These two sectors are very long and generally see the demise of the morning breakaway. After 180 kilometers they wear away at the ardor. It's at Wandignies that Andrea Tafi massacred the peloton in 1999. It's also where he tried another acceleration in 2003. It's also there that Dario Pieri showed all his power in crushing the cobbles."

Mons-en-Pévèle: "Francesco Moser (1978, 1979, 1980) and Sean Kelly (1984, 1986) won Paris–Roubaix here. The winner will be among the first three to leave Mons. It's a very difficult sector that demands power and technique, difficult after 200 kilometers."

L'Arbre: "Here you throw in whatever you have left. It's seen some wonderful duels, such as between Ballerini and Duclos-Lasalle (1993). You can see who has the strength to win. Museeuw rode like a motorbike here while the rest were riding mopeds."

The vélodrome: "It's all the beauty and magic of Paris–Roubaix. A sprinter isn't sure of winning if there's a bunch. The guys have just ridden 260 kilometers and they're worn out. But that's the case for all the classics. Why didn't Petacchi not dominate Milan-San Remo? Why did Hinault beat Moser, De Vlaeminck, Kuiper and van Calster? Because the wind and track craft play a primordial role. Hinault had perfectly mastered all these elements to dominate his rivals. In the end, it's always the most powerful who succeeds."

The *Amis* also repair the cobbles. *Procycling* observed: "An unseasonably warm and sunny afternoon saw several volunteers engaging in some backbreaking toil to make the route slightly safer and more comfortable for cycling's hard men when they roll out of Compiègne, just north of Paris, on April 10.

"The area repaired was a particularly broken and rutted part of the Cysoing sector, which comes 25 kilometers from the finish at the velodrome in Roubaix, and which is dedicated to two-time winner Gilbert Duclos-Lasalle. After prizing out the broken cobbles with picks, crowbars and shovels, a foundation of gravel and sand was put down and new cobbles laid on top. The stones were then pounded flat and coarse sand forced between them to set them fast."

Most races are just races. Paris–Roubaix is different. It wins the hearts of those who know they will never do more than watch it pass from the roadside. Is there another race in the world for which people like that go out and labor for nothing on the road?

To make it better but at the same time to keep it bad. To keep it the Hell of the North.

Index

CPSIA information can be obtained at www.ICGtesting.com
Printed in the USA
BVOW032220050513

319947BV00001B/88/P